Aviation Communication

FTSK

Publikationen des Fachbereichs
Translations-, Sprach- und Kulturwissenschaft
der Johannes Gutenberg-Universität Mainz
in Germersheim

In Verbindung mit
B. Ahrens, H. W. Drescher, D. Huber,
A. F. Kelletat, P. Kupfer, K. P. Müller, W. Pöckl,
N. Salnikow, M. Schreiber und E. Worbs
herausgegeben von Klaus Pörtl

Reihe A - Abhandlungen und Sammelbände

Band 62

Silvia Hansen-Schirra
Karin Maksymski
(eds.)

Aviation Communication

Between Theory and Practice

Bibliographic Information published by the Deutsche Nationalbibliothek
The Deutsche Nationalbibliothek lists this publication in the Deutsche Nationalbibliografie; detailed bibliographic data is available in the internet at http://dnb.d-nb.de.

Cover Design:
© Olaf Gloeckler, Atelier Platen, Friedberg

Library of Congress Cataloging-in-Publication Data

Languages and Cultures above the Clouds: International English between
 Standardization and Everyday Aviation Communication (Conference) (2010 :
 Germersheim, Germany)
 Aviation communication : between theory and practice / Silvia Hansen-Schirra,
 Karin Maksymski (eds.).
   pages cm
 Articles from the conference „Languages and Cultures above the Clouds:
 International English between Standardization and Everyday Aviation Commu-
 nication," held Nov. 4-5, 2010, Johannes Gutenberg University in Germersheim,
 organized in cooperation with Deutsche Flugsicherung GmbH, site Stuttgart,
 Bernhausen/Filderstadt.
 ISBN 978-3-631-62628-3
  1. Aeronautics—Terminology—Congresses. 2. Aeronautics—Communication
 systems—Congresses. 3. English language—Technical English—Congresses.
 4. Intercultural communication—Congresses. I. Hansen, Silvia, 1975- II. Maksymski, Karin, 1982- III. Title.
 TL509.L36 2010
 629.13—dc23
                                                                            2013002516

ISSN 1869-9227
ISBN 978-3-631-62628-3
© Peter Lang GmbH
Internationaler Verlag der Wissenschaften
Frankfurt am Main 2013
All rights reserved.
Peter Lang Edition is an Imprint of Peter Lang GmbH.

Peter Lang – Frankfurt am Main · Berlin · Bruxelles · New York ·
Oxford · Warszawa · Wien

All parts of this publication are protected by copyright. Any
utilisation outside the strict limits of the copyright law, without
the permission of the publisher, is forbidden and liable to
prosecution. This applies in particular to reproductions,
translations, microfilming, and storage and processing in
electronic retrieval systems.

www.peterlang.de

Table of Contents

Preface 7

Importance of language (rules) in aviation

Operational Use of the English Language – ATM Safety around Europe (Dragica Stankovic) 9

Applied Linguistics and Air Traffic Control: Focus on Language Awareness and Intercultural Communication (Markus Bieswanger) 15

Deviation from standard language

Play again, please! – Transcribing Aviation Communication (Wendy L. Fox) .. 33

Linguistic Characteristics of Aviation English and their Practical Use – An Analysis (Silja Koble/Patricia Roh) 43

So much to say, so few Words – Why Pilots deviate from Standard Phraseology (César Holzem) 55

The power of language

"...Words Were Originally Magic..." Constructiv(ist)Thinking about Language with Regard to Incident Investigation (Alice Müller-Leonhardt) 77

Linguistic Dominance in Air Traffic Control (Silvia Hansen-Schirra) 83

Language teaching

The Role of Plain Language in English Training for French Air Traffic Controllers (Lynette Rees) 95

ICAO in Military Air Traffic Control – First Experiences with a New Language Proficiency Examination (Stefan Hinz/Dugald Sturges) 105

Incidents and emergencies

Incident investigation or "What happens when something has happened?" (Helmut Montag/Martina Sahliger) 113

"Declaring Emergency" – A pilot's view (Marcel Mattenberger) 125

Communication Needs in a High Risk Environment (Martina Sahliger/ Ortwin Renn) 131

Preface

This book contains a collection of articles dealing with aviation communication from a practical as well as a theoretical perspective. Its publication arises as a result of the conference "Languages and cultures above the clouds – International English between standardization and everyday aviation communication", which took place on the 4th and 5th November 2010 at the Johannes Gutenberg University in Germersheim. This international conference was organized by Silvia Hansen-Schirra and Martina Sahliger in cooperation with the Deutsche Flugsicherung GmbH (Site Stuttgart, Bernhausen/Filderstadt) and was funded by the Johannes Gutenberg University Mainz (*Inneruniversitäre Forschungsförderung Stufe I*) within the project "Interferences, conflicts and challenges in high risk communication – an empirical study of international aviation communication".

The aim of the conference and, in consequence, also of this book is to promote the dialogue between researchers, operative aviation staff, and (language) trainers – i.e., between the theoretical and practical protagonists of the field. All of them deal with language issues, especially with the standard phraseology developed by the ICAO (International Civil Aviation Organization) in order to make aviation communication more consistent, efficient, and safer. To this end, the following questions have to be addressed:

- Which role do language and language rules in general and (non-native) English in particular play for aviation communication?
- How can the ICAO Standard be applied in every-day practice?
- How do deviations from the standard phraseology affect the daily routine of pilots and controllers?
- How can language training for controllers and pilots be optimized?
- How can these questions be investigated from a linguistic point of view?

Aiming at the first two questions, the first articles deal with the importance of language and standardization in aviation communication. Within this context they are concerned with the status of English as a Lingua Franca in aviation communication and the applicability of ICAO in everyday practice. In particular, Dragica Stankovic discusses the language impact on safety and efficiency in Air Traffic Control (ATC) and introduces EVAIR – the EUROCONTROL Voluntary ATM Incident Reporting. In the second article, Markus Bieswanger investigates problems in intercultural communication and stresses the relevance of language awareness for non-native as well as native speakers of English.

Three complementary articles are dedicated to the analysis of deviations from standard language. Wendy L. Fox draws attention to the comprehension difficulties when listening to, transcribing and analyzing recordings of dialogues between controllers and pilots. She argues that background knowledge is necessary to understand this highly specialized type of communication within its real-life settings. Silja Koble and Patricia Roh present a sample analysis of transcribed dialogues on the basis of which characteristics of aviation English (including deviations from the standard) become clear. From a pilot's perspective, César Holzem names reasons and factors for deviations from ICAO.

Alice Müller-Leonhardt and Silvia Hansen-Schirra approach aviation communication from a theoretical linguistic perspective: both deal with the power of language and the social role relationship between the dialogue partners involved. In her article, Müller-Leonhardt introduces constructivist theories and their possible application when dealing with misunderstandings in incident investigation. In addition, Hansen-Schirra presents a corpus-based analysis of authority and linguistic dominance in ATC.

Where only one, strongly standardized language, i.e. aviation English, should be used in communication, language teaching plays an important role. Therefore Lynette Rees speaks about the role of plain language in English training for non-native controllers discussing the development, implementation and efficiency of language proficiency requirements and courses. In addition to this, Stefan Hinz and Dugald Sturges discuss the language examination procedures and their compliance with ICAO proficiency levels within the context of military ATC.

Finally, the last articles in this book are concerned with incidents and emergencies and their possible relation to language use. Based on the investigation of incidents, Helmut Montag and Martina Sahliger stress the importance of situational awareness and the development of prevention methods. Dealing not only with communicative but also with technical aspects, Marcel Mattenberger explains why and when a pilot has to declare emergency. And to conclude, Martina Sahliger and Ortwin Renn investigate the communication needs in high risk environments and their application in aviation communication.

This book (like the preceding conference) substantiates and prospectively encourages an exchange between pilots, air traffic controllers, (language) trainers and researchers, i.e. an exchange between theory and practice. With this book, we hope to contribute not only to the discussion of communication problems, but also to the development of efficient solutions concerning communication in Air Traffic Control.

Germersheim, September 2011   The Editors

Dragica Stankovic

Operational Use of the English Language –
ATM Safety around Europe

1 Introduction

Aviation represents a domain which arguably more than any other, requires world-wide standardized and harmonized regulations and practices.

As in other activities, common language and communication facilities represent the main means for exercising a job. But it seems that in no other industry is the use of language and communications more critical, and where misunderstandings in pilot-air traffic controller communication is so potentially disastrous, than in air traffic control.

A key mitigation in reducing aviation safety and operational problems is the use of **one** language in accordance with the agreed international standards and recommended practices related to the proficiency of the plain language and proper use of the aviation phraseology.

World common practice and operational and safety reasons have made English the Number One language in aviation, but not the only one. On the operational frequency it is not uncommon to hear two different languages, which could create a problem to those who do not know both of them. The need to have only one language on the operational frequency, when pilots and air traffic controllers communicate, creates a lot of issues among which the most important are: regulation, safety and efficiency but very often followed by historical and political discussions.

The data used in this article to identify language problems in Air Traffic Management (ATM) come from the EUROCONTROL Voluntary ATM Incident Reporting (EVAIR) scheme. EVAIR, which was established five years ago, is the first voluntary ATM incident data collection scheme to be organized on a pan-European level. ATM incidents are provided on a daily basis and are channeled through the Safety Management Systems (SMSs) of the airlines and Air Navigation Service Providers (ANSPs) who participate in the scheme. The data is analyzed by EVAIR experts who are licensed Air Traffic Controllers, pilots and engineers.

2 ATC Operations – Language Impact on Safety and Efficiency

The largest number of the EVAIR incidents come from pilots through the airlines' SMSs. Flying across the whole world every day, pilots have a clear perspective of the knowledge of English language in air traffic control (ATC). The Air Traffic Controllers (ATCOs), on the other hand, have a direct line to the different airlines and their pilots' knowledge of the English language.

EVAIR reports show that language problems are pan-European issues. In the EVAIR data base they fall within air-ground communication[1], which covers Operational (e.g. phraseology) and Spoken (e.g. plain language) communication.

EVAIR data shows that 14.5 % of all incidents have spoken or operational communication as one of the causal issues. The most frequent language problems are:

- Correct application of the ICAO (International Civil Aviation Organization) phraseology and proficiency in the plain English language when phraseology is not sufficient; and
- The use of two languages in a single environment and the problem of pilots' awareness of the traffic situation.

---

[1] According to the Harmonized European Incident Definitions Initiative for ATM (HEIDI) taxonomy air ground communication encompasses:
Operational communication, which covers Air-Ground and Ground-Ground communication, and Use of equipment verification testing. Air-Ground communication encompasses hearback omitted; pilots' readback; standard phraseology; message construction; radio telephony (R/T) monitoring including sector frequency monitoring and emergency frequency monitoring; handling of radio communication failure; and unlawful radio communications transmission. Ground-Ground communication refers to the standard phraseology; speech techniques; message construction; and standard use of equipment like radio frequency, telephones, intercoms, etc.
Spoken communication, which covers human/human communication encompassing Air-Ground and Ground-Ground communications, but also call sign confusion, noise interference and other spoken information provided in plain language. Air-ground communication refers to language/accent; situations not conveyed by pilots; pilots' breach of radio telephony (R/T); workload, misunderstanding/misinterpretation; and other pilot problems. Ground-ground communication refers to misunderstanding/ misinterpretation and poor/no coordination.

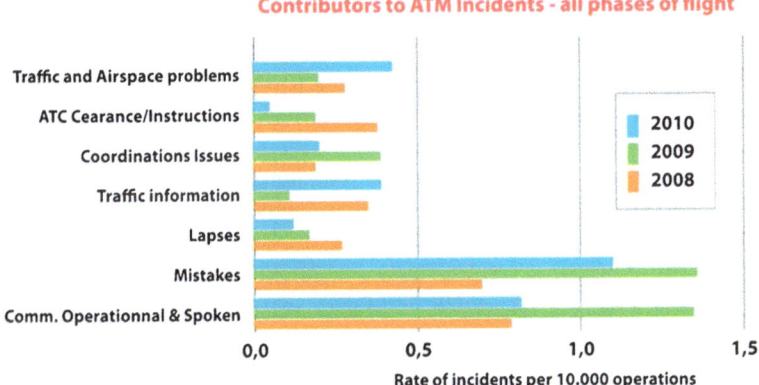

Figure 1: Contributors to incidents, 2008-2010 (EVAIR 2011)

The graph in *Figure 1* shows that through 2008-2010, Operational and Spoken Communication as well as 'Mistakes' were the main causes for incidents. The most frequent events that have language as one of the causes are: Level Bust, Call Sign Confusion, Go-around and Runway and Taxiway Incursion/Excursion.

Within the EVAIR database the areas with the highest number of reports are Standard Phraseology and Proficiency in English and (loss of) Situational awareness due to use of a language (usually the national one) other than English.

2.1 Correct Application of the ICAO Phraseology and Proficiency in a "Common" or Plain Language when Phraseology is not Sufficient

Correct application of the ICAO phraseology and proficiency in a "common" or plain language when phraseology is not sufficient is related to ATCOs and pilots. This does not, however, apply only to those whose mother tongue is not English but also to native-speakers of English. In general, the main problems for non-native speakers of English are a lack of knowledge in phraseology and in plain language, while for those to whom the English language is a mother tongue, the problems are the use of non-standard phraseology and the use of local terms and phrases.

Example: Short summary of an incident with language proficiency as the contributory factor

After take-off, the landing gear lever got stuck. In addition, an engine problem appeared. The pilot requested to be allowed to make a holding pattern due to technical problems. Quality of ATC radio telephone (R/T) communications and English proficiency was quite poor. R/T communication consumed half of the entire time required to solve the technical problem! Assistance came from the company pilot on the jump seat, who spoke the local language.

2.2 The Use of Two Languages in a Single Environment and the Problem of Pilots' Awareness of the Traffic Situation

Pilots' situational awareness of the traffic situation and their active participation in traffic has a significant impact on air traffic safety and efficiency. The EVAIR data shows that the use of two languages in the same airspace is an everyday situation across Europe. It creates safety and air traffic efficiency problems. In such an environment, pilots cannot participate actively in managing the traffic scenario.

National regulation could contribute a lot by supporting the use of the English language as the sole language in aviation communication as the best safety and efficiency solution.

Example: Short summary of an incident with the use of two languages in a single environment and the problem of pilot's situational awareness

The incident occurred with three aircraft; one just landed, the second one was ready for take-off, and the third one was in the approach phase approaching the final. The communication with the landing aircraft was in the national non-English language. After landing the a/c stayed on the runway longer but that was not known to the non-national language speaking pilots. The departing traffic communicated with the ATC in English and got clearance for take-off, which was ATC's mistake. Due to lack of situational awareness, the pilot of the departing traffic accepted the clearance. Take-off was aborted at a speed of 60kts. The third a/c made a Go Around since there were two a/c on the runway. The pilot of the departing traffic stated that if he had been aware of the communication with the landing traffic he would have been in a position to warn ATC and correct the mistake. The use of the national language reduced general awareness and possible correction of the mistake.

3 Regulatory Issues

Two main regulatory issues have been identified through discussions with different Air Navigation Service Providers and airlines, and analysis of the ATM incident reports:

- Application of International Standards and Recommended Practices (SARPs) and improvement on the training field; and
- Status of the English language as the aviation language in national regulation.

3.1 Application of International Standards and Recommended Practices

It is generally acknowledged that, for a number of reasons – historical, cultural and political – the level of knowledge of English in the world varies considerably. In that regard the need to define a minimum proficiency in English language for aviation communication is recognized as being of great importance.

The main priorities, in that regard, should be the establishment of English as the common language for international aviation communication and the full application of ICAO standards for proficiency in English in pronunciation, structure, vocabulary, fluency, comprehension and interaction.

The percentage of incidents caused by language in the EVAIR database provides unambiguous support of the above statements and also of the necessity of English as the sole language for international aeronautical communication at airports and in the airspace designated for use by international air services.

3.2 Status of the English Language in National Regulation

Political and cultural reasons could create obstacles for the use of English as the single language in airspace designated for international use. In a number of states across the world, the use of English in aviation communication is not regulated by national regulation or if it is, then national language has the same priority as English. This is the origin of various problems.

As the best solution from a safety and efficiency point of view, Airline associations support practices in national policies to use the English language as the only one at airports and in the airspace designated for use by international air services. Unfortunately, at the moment it is not possible, in some areas, for political reasons which require further work, to improve the situation within the current circumstances and to make plans for the future. One of the possible solutions is that future pilots and air traffic controllers, as a precondition to participate in the selection process, should already possess a high level of English.

The practice shows that there are significant varieties amongst states in this respect. On the one hand, some states do have high standards regarding the knowledge of English as a prerequisite for applicants to enter the selection procedure. Usually this is a level of proficiency in spoken English. On the other hand, there are states which do not have any requirements or, if they do, it is knowledge of one foreign language, which may not necessarily be English.

There is a need for standardized requirements implemented in national regulation related to the applicants' knowledge of English as a condition to enter the selection procedure for pilots and air traffic controllers.

3.3 Maintaining and Upgrading the Knowledge of the English Language

Improvements in the training field, refresher courses and periodic checks could bring positive results and ensure an appropriate level of English language knowledge. Special attention should be paid to R/T phraseology but also to proficiency in plain language, as phraseology alone cannot satisfy all communication requirements. This should concern both those to whom English is a foreign language but also to whom English is a mother tongue. Certainly the content of the courses for these two different categories should be different.

National regulations differ in various states with regard to maintaining and improving the knowledge of English. In some states refresher courses as well as continuous checks are required by national regulations while in others there are no more language checks or refresher courses after obtaining the initial license. In the current situation, more work and harmonization is needed.

The author works as a manager of the EVAIR (EUROCONTROL Voluntary ATM Incident Reporting) function.

References

EVAIR (2011): "EVAIR Safety Bulletin No 6. Summer Periods April-September", in http://www.ukfsc.co.uk/files/Safety%20Briefings%20_%20 Presentations/ATM%20%20EVAIR%20bulletin%2006%20Posted%20June %202011.pdf [2008-2010 Evolution].

http://www.eurocontrol.int/safety/public/standard_page/evair.html

Markus Bieswanger

Applied Linguistics and Air Traffic Control:
Focus on Language Awareness and Intercultural Communication

1 Introduction

Over the past half century, the scope of Applied Linguistics has broadened from its original focus on matters related to language teaching and learning to a "problem-oriented and problem-solving field" dealing "with the theoretical and empirical investigation of real world problems in which language and communication are a central issue" (Knapp/Antos 2007-2011: back cover; for a historical overview of the development of Applied Linguistics cf. Bieswanger 2007: 402-407). Along the same lines, Cook (2003: 20) defined Applied Linguistics as "the academic discipline concerned with the relation of knowledge about language and decision making in the real world." This means that many of the current issues and problems connected with real life communications between air traffic controllers (ATCs) and pilots are at the heart of contemporary Applied Linguistics. With respect to the use of English in aviation contexts (cf. Bieswanger/ Intemann forthcoming), aspects such as the development of unambiguous phraseology, the definition of proficiency levels as well as English language training and testing of controllers and pilots fall just as much within the scope of Applied Linguistics as do other relevant issues such as language variation and diversity, multilingualism, the use of English as a Lingua Franca, language awareness and intercultural communication. Due to space constraints, many of these areas can only be touched upon here. This paper will focus primarily on aspects of language awareness and intercultural communication in voice-based air traffic control communications and present observations based on authentic controller-pilot communications. All transcripts are based on audio recordings from JFK International Airport in New York, United States, taken from the archives of www.liveatc.net.

2 Language Awareness and Air Traffic Control

In the constitution of the *Association for Language Awareness*, language awareness is defined as "explicit knowledge about language, and conscious perception and sensitivity in language learning, language teaching and language use" (quoted in Garret/James 2000: 330). In the context of air traffic control, it is particularly conscious perception and sensitivity in language use that is instrumental in facilitating effective and efficient communication between ATCs and pilots from different linguistic backgrounds. This includes communication in English between native speakers of different languages as well as communication between native speakers of different varieties of English.

When English-based controller-pilot communications fail in situations involving non-native speakers of English, native speakers and the media in countries of the so-called *inner circle* – i.e. countries where English is traditionally the primary language and the first or dominant language of the majority of the population (cf. Kachru 1985: 12) – are often quick to blame the allegedly inadequate command of the English language of a non-native speaker (see below). Indeed, insufficient English language proficiency has been identified by accident investigators as a contributing factor, leading to the loss of more than one thousand lives in several collisions and crashes (Mathews 2004a; cf. also Feldman 1998; Jones 2003: 237-239; Intemann 2008: 71). In response to these accidents, the 32nd Session of the ICAO Assembly in 1998 decided to address the matter of English language proficiency in aviation communications (ICAO 2010: vii), focusing on non-native speakers of English. As a result, the ICAO Council adopted amendments to *Annex 1: Personnel Licensing, Annex 6: Operation of Aircraft, Annex 10: Aeronautical Telecommunications, Annex 11: Air Traffic Services* and the *Procedures for Air Navigation Services: Air Traffic Management* on March 5, 2003, strengthening and extending English language proficiency requirements in international aviation and demanded their implementation by March 5, 2008 (cf., e.g., Mathews 2004b: 4; ICAO 2007a: 2). However, while gladly acknowledging the obvious need for the implementation of such proficiency requirements, it is certainly worth emphasizing that the lack of language awareness on the part of a number of controllers and pilots who are native speakers of English adversely affects effective and efficient controller-pilot communications as well. The examples of authentic interactions between ATCs and flight crews presented in the following subsections will illustrate this claim.

2.1 JFK Tower and Aerogal 700

In September 2010, an incident involving Aerolíneas Galápagos (AeroGal) flight 700 from Guayaquil, Ecuador, to JFK International Airport (JFK), United States, made headline news (ABC 7 New York 2010; Aviation Herald 2010, see also *Figure 1*).

Figure 1: Screenshot, ABC 7, New York 2010

The two parallel runways 13 Left and 13 Right were both in use at JFK on September 19, 2010 when Aerogal flight 700 (GLG 700) received a landing clearance for 13 Left from the controller working the JFK Tower position at the time:[1]

JFK Tower:	Aerogal seven hundred heavy Kennedy Tower (.) winds calm (.) runway one three left (.) cleared to land [200 words per minute]
(0.6 seconds)	
GLG 700:	wind calm (.) one three left (.) cleared to land Aerogal seven (hundred) heavy [262 words per minute]

Transcript 1: GLG 700 landing clearance and readback

The instructions given by the American controller were delivered at a speed of precisely 200 words per minute. In Volume 2 of *Annex 10 to the Convention on International Civil Aviation* (1944), i.e. the annex dealing with aeronautical telecommunications, the ICAO recommends "an even rate of speech not exceeding 100 words per minute" (ICAO 2001: Section 5.2.1.5.3; cf. also ICAO 2006: Section 2.2). There has been some debate as to whether the recommended speech rate may be too slow; for example, Cauldwell (2007: n.p.) considers 100 words per minute "an uncomfortable, unrealistically slow speed of speech." However, fast-paced speech is generally problematic in high risk environments in which details are crucial, particularly in communicative situations involving speakers from different linguistic backgrounds and during phases of high

---

[1] Transcript symbols adapted from Jefferson (2004: 24-31); (.) a dot in parentheses indicates a brief interval within utterances; (word) parenthesized words are dubious; ( ) empty parentheses in the transcript indicate unintelligible passages.

cognitive workload, such as the approach phase of a flight. In fact, very high rates of speech have been shown to cause problems in actual pilot-controller communication (Bieswanger/Intemann 2008). Despite the high speed of delivery in this example, the pilot of GLG 700 in charge of communications with air traffic control did not seem to have much trouble with the transmission, since the clearance given by the ATC was a part of routine operations and contained several pauses enhancing understandability. Consequently, the pilot gave a full readback of the instructions only 0.6 seconds later, acknowledging the clearance to land on runway 13 Left.

About one minute after the landing clearance had been issued, the pilot of Delta flight 122, waiting for departure from runway 13 Right, warned the Tower controller: "Tower for Delta one two two (.) looks like that guy is trying to land on runway one three right." Runway 13 Right, however, was occupied by a Jetblue regional jet that had just started its takeoff roll. The controller immediately instructed GLG 700 to go around:

JFK Tower:	Aerogal seven hundred heavy (.) go around (.) fly runway heading because you are lining up for the wrong runway (.) you need to start an immediate right turn [252 words per minute]
(0.9 seconds)	
GLG 700:	okay roger going around Aerogal seven (hundred) heavy [168 words per minute]

Transcript 2: GLG 700 go around instruction and readback

The interspeaker pause time, i.e. the time elapsed between the instruction given by the ATC, delivered at an extremely high speed of 252 words per minute, and the response by the pilot of GLG 700, given at a speech rate of 168 words per minute, was 0.9 seconds and thus 50 % longer than during the routine situation in Transcript 1. In a television interview with ABC, the controller said that "the Aerogal jet seemed to hesitate" (ABC 7 New York 2010). As a reaction to the perceived hesitation, the ATC repeated the instruction to turn right immediately after GLG 700 had acknowledged the go around:

JFK Tower:	but you need to start an immediate right turn you need to turn right (.) there is somebody rolling underneath you [222 words per minute]
(1.1 seconds)	
GLG 700:	roger (…) heading
JFK Tower:	[*stepped on*] heading one eight zero for now

Transcript 3: GLG 700 repetition of instruction to turn right

Similarly to the controller's instruction to go around (see Transcript 2), the repetition of the command to turn right in Transcript 3 was delivered at a very high speech rate of 222 words per minute and almost without pauses. The time elapsed between the command and the readback increased again to 1.1 seconds.

While it has to be pointed out that there is no doubt about the fact that the pilots of GLG 700 made a serious mistake by approaching a runway for which they did not have a landing clearance and which was in use by another aircraft, a close analysis of the ensuing communications allows us to draw a number of conclusions concerning a lack of language awareness on the part of the native-speaking controller.

As soon as the controller was made aware of the imminent danger, the rate of speech increased to an extremely high speed of 252 words per minute (see Transcript 2). Additionally, the command to go around is followed by two conflicting instructions concerning the direction, namely *fly runway heading* and *you need to start an immediate right turn*, as well as a wordy explanation of the reason for the go around. The controller also switched almost completely from standardized phraseology, which pilots are probably most familiar with, to plain and colloquial English, which is much more difficult to understand for non-native speakers. Since the pilot of GLG 700 had earlier been able to read the landing clearance back without any major difficulties (see Transcript 1), the alleged hesitation and the delayed response of the pilot of GLG 700 may not have necessarily or even exclusively been related to a lack of proficiency in English. The high speech rate of the controller, the use of plain English as well as the conflicting and unnecessary information included in the go around instruction most likely also played a role.

In Transcript 3, the delivery of the repetition of the instruction to turn right at a still very high speech rate of 222 words per minute is not the only indication of a lack of crucial language awareness on the part of the controller, i.e. insufficient sensitivity in language use to convey the message as effectively and efficiently as possible. The almost complete absence of pauses, the repeated use of the wordy and colloquial construction *you need to*, the lengthy explanation *there is somebody rolling underneath you* and the lack of information concerning a heading, which seems to confuse the pilot even further, point in the same direction. The ATC said in the TV interview with ABC: "I need to as quickly as possible get it into this man's head you need to turn your airplane or he's going to climb into the bottom of you" (ABC 7 New York 2010). It has been reported before that perceived and/or real time pressure may lead to an increased speech rate in air traffic control communication. With regard to such situations, Silberstein/Dietrich (2003: 9) quote an ATC who said about himself: "I talk faster, a lot faster – I talk so fast that they have to slow me down because they don't understand me anymore." However, the need for a quick effect, as acknowledged by the controller involved in the GLG 700 incident, should not automatically translate into an increased speech rate and the repeated use of colloquial sequences which seem to be ineffective. Most likely, a much slower delivery of the instructions at the beginning of both Transcripts 2 and 3 as well as shorter, less complex and less colloquial transmissions would have been more efficient and effective. A clear command such as *go around (.) turn right immediately* or *go around (.) heading one eight zero immediately*, even if delivered at the recommended speech rate of 100 words per minute, would have taken less time, would have been easier to understand and would have probably achieved an effect more quickly than the wordy instruction given by the ATC at the beginning of Transcript 2. The explanation of the reasons for the go around could have been left for later.

The incident was discussed in several online aviation forums and a number of contributors identified an alleged lack of proficiency in English, on the part of the non-native speaking pilots of GLG 700, as one of the problems. As part of an explanation why GLG 700 did not respond to the instruction to go around more quickly, a contributor to a discussion of the incident in the *Civil Aviation* forum on www.airliners.net on Oct 1, 2010, wrote: "[...] when you are tired (long flight), unfamiliar and English is not your native language, things in aviation happen very, very quick". Just three replies later, another user who identifies himself as *American* and is thus very likely a native speaker of English quotes the passage "English is not your native language, things in aviation happen very, very quick" from the previous post and adds the following comment:

> Which is why there needs to be more emphasis on actually understanding the English language than just being able to speak it. You could probably teach a monkey how to speak English, but he wouldn't understand it. **These people need to understand English,** so that situations like this don't get worse than it was. [signature deleted] (www.airliners.net, October 1, 2010; my emphasis)

This quotation illustrates the assumption of many native speakers of English that non-native speakers and an allegedly inadequate proficiency in English are, almost by default, responsible for problems in English-based controller-pilot communication. The quotation as a whole and particularly the highlighted passage *These people need to understand English* also shows a derogatory attitude towards non-native speakers of English. When a user in the *ATC/Pilot Audio Clips* forum on liveatc.net on Sept 28, 2010, dared to suggest to also look at the role of the ATC in this incident, another user replied: "[...] And you question his action??? You want to 'look at' HIS role? His role is simple. It's spelled H-E-R-O. [...]" (www.liveatc.net, September 30, 2010).

Native speakers often assume a certain linguistic infallibility of the native speaker(s) in communication situations involving native and non-native speakers, reflecting the widespread but false perception of native speakers as being the "owners" of the language. Concerning the alleged "ownership" of English by the native speakers of the language, the *Manual on the Implementation of ICAO Language Proficiency Requirements* explicitly states: "In the modern world of global communication, and particularly in the case of the English language, this point of view is becoming difficult to defend" (ICAO 2010: Section 2.4.1.3; for a similar perspective cf., e.g., Graddol 1997; Seidlhofer 2008). In the same document, it is also made clear that "[n]ative speakers of English, in particular, have an ethical obligation to increase their linguistic awareness and to take special care in the delivery of messages" (ICAO 2010: Section 5.3.1.3). Additionally, native speakers of English also have to be made aware that English-based communications in air traffic control contexts are, for the most part, a specialization based on the natural English language but are not identical with it. This includes the awareness that the speech rate has to be reduced to a reasonable pace in all transmissions. However, Bieswanger/Intemann (2008) found that high speech rates of up to 260 words per minute are fairly common at JFK. Even a probably well-meant reduction of the speech rate of some ATCs when communicating with non-native speakers of English does not fully solve the problem. Such "speed switching" makes it difficult for non-native English-speaking pilots to obtain and maintain situational awareness[2] during fast-paced transmissions between native speakers. Fast-paced transmissions and speed switching by native speakers adversely affect the situational awareness of non-native speakers of English, just like language switching to unfamiliar languages adversely affects the situational awareness of native English-speaking pilots abroad (Prinzo/ Campbell/Hendrix 2010: 26-27). The incident involving GLG 700 and JFK Tower discussed in this section shows that native speakers do not only have an ethical but also a functional obligation to take special care in the delivery of messages.

2.2 JFK Ground and Etihad 503

Another example of insufficient language awareness on the part of a native speaker of English involved in controller-pilot communications is the following conversation between JFK Ground and the pilot of flight Etihad 503 (ETD 503) (October 27, 2006):

---

[2] In aviation contexts, "[s]ituational awareness involves conscious recognition of all the factors and conditions – operational, technical and human – which affect the safe operation of an aircraft" (CAA 2006: 2). For pilots, situational awareness is thus derived from a whole range of information, including knowledge about the positions and intentions of other aircraft and vehicles in the vicinity of one's own aircraft.

JFK Ground:	echo india (.) echo tango (delta) five o three where do you park?
ETD 503:	bravo twenty eight Sir
JFK Ground:	what taxiway? the letter!
ETD 503:	oh negative Sir we are on two two right holding short of foxtrot
JFK Ground:	**what taxiway do you enter the ramp?**
ETD 503:	okay Sir we just exit the runway and we are holding short of foxtrot on two two right
JFK Ground:	you are not listening to what I am asking you (.) **what taxiway do you enter the ramp?**
ETD 503:	I'm not on the ramp yet Sir
JFK Ground:	**what taxiway do you enter the ramp?** tell me! (.) what letter?
ETD 503:	okay we can enter at kilo for (.) Etihad five zero three
JFK Ground:	that is what I need to get out of you we talk like six times (.) straight ahead and hold short of hotel Sir
ETD 503:	straight ahead hold short of hotel roger

Transcript 4: JFK Ground vs. ETD 503; my emphasis

Some pilots who are unfamiliar with the taxi procedures at JFK are confused by the somewhat unusual situation that ground control asks for the taxiway needed to get to the final parking position. In this example, the pilot of ETD 503, who was otherwise fluent in English, was obviously not able to understand the intention of the controller's question. After unsuccessfully asking *what taxiway?*, the controller asked the exact same question *what taxiway do you enter the ramp?* three more times, with increased agitation and without giving any explanations or making any attempt to rephrase. It is, however, precisely this ability to make the necessary adjustments to the way we express ourselves which makes up an important component of language awareness. Native speakers have to be made aware that meaning in human interaction is not simply transferred but has to be negotiated by the interlocutors (cf. Allwright 1999: 230).

The examples in this section show that an increased language awareness of native speakers of English is a prerequisite for effective and efficient communications, as is the implementation of proficiency standards for non-native speakers. Unfortunately, native speakers and the authorities in native English-speaking countries do not always see the need for an increase in language awareness, often at least partly because the necessary separation between English as a natural language and the use of English in air traffic control is not explicitly made. In many countries of the inner circle of Englishes, the effective use of English in aviation contexts is taken for granted. For example, the *Aeronautical Aviation Publication* states that "[t]he U.S. does not require Air traffic controllers or aeronautical station operators to demonstrate the ability to speak and understand the language" (FAA 2009: Section GEN 1.7) as required by Section 1.2.9.2 of *Annex 1: Personnel Licensing* (ICAO 2006).

While particularly important in communication between native speakers and non-native speakers of English, increased language awareness is also beneficial in other situations including native-native communication. The following complaint of a British Airways pilot, most likely a native speaker of English, to an American controller at JFK, also most likely a native speaker of English, illustrates this point impressively (December 11, 2003): "I'm sorry (.) I'm very new and you say it so quickly and in such a strange accent I just don't understand."

3 Intercultural Communication and Air Traffic Control

The other aspect addressed in this paper, which is closely related to language awareness, is the role of intercultural communication in air traffic control communications. Most simply defined, intercultural communication is "concerned with communication across cultures" (Spencer-Oatey/Kotthoff 2007: 1) or more specifically with communication between people with different cultural backgrounds (cf. *Journal of Intercultural Communication*: "Policy Statement" at http://www.immi.se/intercultural/). A more precise definition of *intercultural communication* is difficult, because culture is an extremely complex social concept and the term *culture* "means many different things to different people" (Gudykunst/Kim 2003: 14). However, many of us have a fairly straightforward idea of what constitutes culture and would agree that "shared values, attitudes, beliefs, behaviors, [and] norms" (McDaniel/Samovar/Porter 2008: 10) are among the central aspects. While "[i]t is now widely accepted that cultures cannot simply be reduced to nationality" (Spencer-Oatey/Kotthoff 2007: 7), the boundaries between cultures at the societal level do in fact often coincide with political boundaries (Gudykunst/Kim 2003: 17). This means that due to the international character of aviation, much controller-pilot interaction is inherently intercultural communication.

Based on our own cultural background, we have certain expectations concerning appropriate communication behavior of others and make predictions about the effects of our own communication behavior. Particularly when communicating with people from a different cultural background, these expectations are not always met and our predictions sometimes turn out to be wrong. This can lead to irritation on the part of one interlocutor or all interlocutors, often impairing effective and efficient communication. The outcome of such a situation can be observed in the following transcript, which is a continuation of the conversation between JFK Ground and ETD 503 discussed in Section 2 (see Transcript 4). During the previous conversation, the controller had been repeatedly asking the same question *What taxiway do you enter the ramp?* with increasing agitation and had given direct orders such as *Tell me!* and *The letter!* (see Transcript 4):

JFK Ground:	E T D [sic!] five o three follow Asiana at golf hold short of juliet on the runway
ETD 503:	ah yes we follow the Asiana and next time I would like you to be polite with me (.) thank you
JFK Ground	okay [*briefly stepped on*] if I gotta talk to you six times and I got other people I gotta talk to (.) and you don't understand what I'm saying
ETD 503:	[*stepped on*] what I'm saying (.) polite with me alright

Transcript 5: ETD 503 complains about perceived impoliteness of JFK Ground

The pilot of ETD 503 obviously felt that the controller had previously violated the rules of politeness by not paying him as much respect as he had expected. In terms of politeness theory, the perceived lack of respect by the controller had threatened the pilot's face, i.e. the controller had committed a face-threatening act (cf. Brown/Levinson 1987: 61-83). While the concept of *face* – a notion closely related to the English folk term *face* used in expressions such as *losing face* – has been claimed to be universal, Brown/Levinson (1987: 61) explicitly state that "the content of face will differ in different cultures". In other words, what threatens a person's face in one culture does not necessarily threaten it in another culture, and what is necessary to maintain a person's face in a conversation, i.e. what is considered appropriate to meet a person's *face needs* (cf. Myers-Scotton 2006: 193), may very well differ considerably between cultures.

In our example, the pilot's personal and cultural background had led him to expect more respect from the controller. The repeated use of the same question with increasing agitation and without any attempt of an explanation as well as the direct orders given by the controller had obviously not met the pilot's expectations and face needs. The difference in perspective between the pilot and the controller is most likely, among other things, related to different views of the pilot profession in the United States and many other parts of the world. For example, according to a *forsa* poll concerning the prestige of 29 occupations conducted in Germany in 2009, pilots were considered the third most prestigious group (Bundesleitung dbb 2009: 18). Pilots were only outranked by firefighters and nurses, but ranked higher than doctors and judges. In contrast, the *Harris Poll* of the same year on the prestige of professions in the United States did not even include *pilot* among the 23 occupations on the list (HarrisInteractive 2009). With reference to the United States, it is frequently suggested that the status of the pilot profession has declined dramatically over the past decades. In 2009, the author of an article about Captain Sullenberger in the *New York Magazine* claims that "piloting has become anything but glamorous" (Kolker 2009) and provides a number of quotations to back up his point of view:

'Twenty-five years ago, we were a step below astronauts,' says one veteran pilot. 'Now we're a step above bus drivers. And the bus drivers have a better pension.' [...] 'Pilots are being treated as a commodity,' says Gary Hummel, training committee chairman for the U.S. Airline Pilots Association. (Kolker 2009)

What do these differences in prestige mean for our example? On the one hand, at least partly due to his cultural background, the ATC was most likely unaware of the level of respect the pilot expected from him. On the other hand, the pilot was probably unaware of the different situation in the United States. Within their own cultural frameworks, both the controller and the pilot felt that their communicative behavior was appropriate. Across cultures, however, the lack of awareness of each other's expectations led to inefficient and ineffective communication. A sizable amount of time was wasted and, due to the discussion of different views on politeness, there was no readback of the crucial instruction to *hold short of juliet* (see Transcript 5).

The case presented here is just one example of a situation in which a lack of awareness of different cultural backgrounds adversely affects controller-pilot communications. Since awareness of one's own culture as well as awareness of the potential and actual differences from other cultures is essential for successful communication across cultures, cultural awareness is often considered to be part of language awareness (cf. Edmondson 2009: 165). It is, of course, impossible to know every detail about all the cultures you could ever come into contact with. Instead, a structured knowledge of areas of potential differences between cultures helps to build cultural awareness (cf., e.g., Myers-Scotton 2006: 186-206). There can be no doubt that the provision of cultural awareness training for all participants in international controller-pilot communications would improve the overall efficiency and effectiveness of such interaction.

4 Conclusion(s)

Effective and efficient communication between air traffic control personnel and flight crews is a prerequisite for safe and efficient air traffic management (ATM). Consequently, "[c]ommunication is one human element that is receiving renewed attention" (ICAO 2010: Foreword). In recent years, one of the major steps towards improved air traffic control communication in international services was the introduction of strengthened provisions for English language proficiency, mainly focusing on non-native speakers of English. The examples presented in this paper illustrate that language awareness and intercultural competence, or a lack thereof, are two additional important factors that influence the effectiveness and efficiency of communication in air traffic control contexts. These factors apply to both native speakers and non-native speakers of English. With respect to native speakers of English, it has been shown that conscious perception and sensitivity in the use of one's native language are instrumental in successful communication between speakers with different linguistic backgrounds. Thus, language awareness has to be addressed in the training and retraining of all personnel involved in air traffic control communication. The need for specific training also holds true for the raising of cultural awareness, because international aviation is inseparably connected with contact between culturally diverse people in ATM and insufficient intercultural competence adversely affects the effectiveness and efficiency of air traffic control communication.

In addition to providing expertise in the areas of language awareness and intercultural competence to the stakeholders involved in ATM, Applied Linguistics can make a valuable contribution to many other aspects of air traffic control communication. Among other things, linguists have long been and should continue to be involved in the development and improvement of standardized phraseologies for aeronautical radiotelephony communications. The increased availability of authentic audio material via the Internet allows researchers to analyze unsuccessful as well as successful air traffic control communication. Their observations are certainly instrumental in providing input to the ATM stakeholders in order to facilitate a further reduction of language- and communication-related problems. Applied linguists could also help to identify and propose solutions for issues such as phonetically similar aircraft identifications and similar sounding waypoints in the same airspace (cf. also Stankovic 2010). And last but not least, the aviation community can greatly benefit from the enormous experience of applied linguists in the traditional core areas of the field. These consist of all matters related to language learning, teaching and assessment, including the discussion and definition of norms and standards as well as the development of proficiency scales (cf. Council of Europe 2001). As mentioned in the introduction to this paper, Applied Linguistics is "the academic discipline concerned with the relation of knowledge about language and decision making in the real world" (Cook 2003: 20) and can thus assist air traffic controllers, pilots and the authorities in making the skies even safer.

Markus Bieswanger is Professor of English Linguistics at the University of Bayreuth, Germany. He has a long-standing research interest in communication in air traffic control contexts, primarily working with authentic audio material.

References

ABC 7 New York (2010): "Eyewitness News Investigation, September 29, 2010: Air Traffic Controller speaks out after 'Close Call'", in: http://abclocal.go.com/wabc/story?section=news/investigators&id=7697310 [29.09.2010].

Allwright, R.L. (1999): "Negotiation of meaning", in: Johnson, Keith / Helen Johnson (ed.): *Encyclopedic Dictionary of Applied Linguistics*. Malden at al.: Blackwell, 230.

Aviation Herald (2010): "Incident: Aerogal B763 at New York on Sep 19th 2010, approached wrong runway", in: http://avherald.com/h?article=431385e9&opt=0 [21.09.2010].

Bieswanger, Markus (2007): "Language and Education", in: Hellinger, Marlis / Anne Pauwels (ed.): *Handbooks of Applied Linguistics, Vol. 9: Handbook of Language and Communication: Diversity and Change*. Berlin/New York: de Gruyter, 401-427.

Bieswanger, Markus/Frauke Intemann (2008): "Between standard and chaos: Aviation English (mis-) communication at JFK International Airport". Paper presented at the *15th World Congress of Applied Linguistics (AILA) 2008*, Essen, Germany.

Bieswanger, Markus/Frauke Intemann (forthcoming): "Aviation English", in: de Bot, Kes/Konrad Schröder/Dieter Wolff (ed.): *English as a Foreign Language: An International Handbook*. Berlin/New York: de Gruyter.

Brown, Penelope/Stephen C. Levinson (1987): *Politeness: Some Universals in Language Usage*. Cambridge at al.: Cambridge University Press.

Bundesleitung dbb – Bundesleitung des dbb Beamtenbund und Tarifunion (2009): *Bürgerbefragung öffentlicher Dienst 2009: Einschätzungen, Erfahrungen und Erwartungen*. Berlin: dbb.

CAA (2006): *Crew Resource Management (CRM) Training. Guidance for Flight Crew, CRM Instructors (CRMIS) and CRM Instructor-Examiners (CRMIES)*. Published by TSO (The Stationery Office) on behalf of the UK Civil Aviation Authority. http://www.caa.co.uk/docs/33/CAP737.PDF [24.10.2011].

Cauldwell, Richard T. (2007): "Defining Fluency for Air Traffic Control", in: http://www.speechinaction.net [January 15, 2011].

Convention on International Civil Aviation (1944): *Convention on International Civil Aviation done at the 7th Day of December 1944*. Original version available at http://www.icao.int/icaonet/arch/doc/7300/7300_orig.pdf, [January 15, 2011].

Cook, Guy (2003) *Applied Linguistics*. Oxford: Oxford University Press.

Council of Europe (2001): *Common European Framework of Reference for Languages: Learning, Teaching, Assessment*. Cambridge: Cambridge University Press.

Edmondson, Willis (2009): "Language Awareness", in: Knapp, Karlfried/Barbara Seidlhofer (eds.): *Handbooks of Applied Linguistics, Vol. 6: Handbook of Foreign Language Communication and Learning*. Berlin/New York: de Gruyter, 163-190.

FAA (Federal Aviation Administration) (2009): *Aeronautical Information Publication*, 20th edition. US Department of Transportation.

Feldman, Joan M. (1998): "Speaking with one voice", *Air Transport World 11*, 43-51.

Garrett, Peter/Carl James (2000): "Language Awareness", in: Byram, Michael (ed.): *The Routledge Encyclopedia of Language Teaching and Learning*. London: Routledge, 330-333.

Graddol, David (1997): *The Future of English? A Guide to Forecasting the Popularity of the English Language in the 21st Century*. London: The British Council.

Gudykunst, William B./Young Yun Kim (2003): *Communicating with Strangers: An Approach to Intercultural Communication*. 4th edition. Boston et al.: McGraw-Hill.

HarrisInteractive (2009): "Firefighters, scientists and doctors seen as most prestigious occupations", in: http://www.harrisinteractive.com/vault/Harris-Interactive-Poll-Research-Pres-Occupations-2009-08.pdf [January 15, 2011].

ICAO (International Civil Aviation Organization) (2001): *Annex 10: Aeronautical Telecommunications. Volume II*, 6th edition.

ICAO (International Civil Aviation Organization) (2006): *Annex 1: Personnel Licencing*. 10th edition.

ICAO (International Civil Aviation Organization) (2007a): *ICAO Assembly – 36th Session: Working Paper on Language Proficiency Requirements*. ICAO Document A36-WP/151.

ICAO (International Civil Aviation Organization) (2007b): *Manual of Radiotelephony*, 4th edition. ICAO Document 9432-AN/925.

ICAO (International Civil Aviation Organization) (2010): *Manual on the Implementation of ICAO Language Proficiency Requirements*. 2nd edition. ICAO Document 9835-AN/453.

Intemann, Frauke (2008): "'Taipei ground, confirm your last transmission was in English... ?' – An Analysis of Aviation English as a World Language", in: Gnutzmann, Claus/Frauke Intemann (ed.): *The Globalisation of English and the English Language Classroom*, 2nd edition. Tübingen: Narr, 76-93.

Jefferson, Gail (2004): "Glossary of Transcript Symbols with an Introduction", in: Lerner, Gene H. (ed.), *Conversation Analysis: Studies from the first generation*. Amsterdam/Philadelphia: Benjamins, 13-31.

Jones, R. Kent (2003): "Miscommunication between Pilots and Air Traffic Control", *Language Problems and Language Planning 27 (3)*, 233-248.

Kachru, Braj B. (1985): "Standards, Codification and Sociolinguistic Realism: The English Language in the Outer Circle", in: Quirk, Randolph/H.G. Widdowson (ed.): *English in the World: Teaching and Learning the Language and Literatures*. Cambridge et al.: Cambridge University Press, 11-30.

Knapp, Karlfried/Gerd Antos (ed.) (2007-2011): *Handbooks of Applied Linguistics*. 9 volumes. Berlin/New York: Mouton de Gruyter.

Kolker, Robert (2009): "'My Aircraft' – Why Sully may be the Last of his Kind", *New York Magazine* February 9, 2009.

Mathews, Elizabeth (2004a): "The Role of Language in Aviation Communications", in: ICAO (ed.): *ICAO Aviation Language Symposium. CD-ROM.* Montreal: ICAO.

Mathews, Elizabeth (2004b): "New Provisions for English Language Proficiency are expected to improve Aviation Safety", *ICAO Journal 59 (1),* 4-6, 27.

McDaniel, Edwin R. / Larry A. Samovar / Richard E. Porter (2008): "Understanding Intercultural Communication: The Working Principles", in: Samovar, Larry A. / Richard E. Porter / Edwin R. McDaniel (ed.): *Intercultural Communication: A Reader.* 12th edition. Boston: Wadsworth Cengage, 6-17.

Myers-Cotton, Carol (2006): *Multiple Voices: An Introduction to Bilingualism.* Malden et al.: Blackwell.

Prinzo, Veronika O./Alan Campbell/Alfred M. Hendrix (2010): *U.S. Airline Transport Pilot International Flight Language Experiences. Report 4: Non-Native English Speaking Controllers Speaking with Native English-Speaking Pilots.* Technical Report DOT/FAA/AM-10/12. Washington, DC: Federal Aviation Administration, Office of Aerospace Medicine.

Seidlhofer, Barbara (2008): "Standard Future or Half-Baked Quackery? Descriptive and Pedagogical Bearings on the Globalisation of English", in: Gnutzmann, Claus/Frauke Intemann (ed.): *The Globalisation of English and the English Language Classroom,* 2nd edition Tübingen: Narr, 159-173.

Silberstein, Dagmar/Rainer Dietrich (2003): "Cockpit Communication under High Cognitive Workload", in: Dietrich, Rainer (ed.): *Communication in High Risk Environments.* Hamburg: Buske.

Spencer-Oatey, Helen/Helga Kotthoff (2007): "Introduction", in: Kotthoff, Helga / Helen Spencer-Oatey (ed.): *Handbooks of Applied Linguistics, Vol. 7: Handbook of Intercultural Communication.* Berlin/New York: de Gruyter, 1-6.

Stankovic, Dragica (2010): "Eurocontrol Voluntary ATM Incident Reporting (EVAIR)". Paper presented at the Eurocontrol & IATA Workshop *Is SMS just paper work? Or a practical instrument to manage the risk!* Brussels, Belgium.

http://www.airliners.net

http://www.immi.se/intercultural/

http://www.liveatc.net

Wendy L. Fox

Play Again, Please!
–
Transcribing Aviation Communication

1 Introduction

This article describes how aviation communication was transcribed to make use of it for further analysis. The problems that occurred during the transcription process and possible solutions illustrate very well where, in general, problems in aviation communication can occur and how they could be avoided or solved.

The transcription was carried out within a project on the analysis of aviation communication. This project focuses on a specific area of aviation communication, namely that which occurs in the immediate airspace around airports. Here, the higher frequency of aircrafts, the higher flight density and the resulting stress for the communication partners offers interesting research possibilities.

We chose Paris-Orly Airport and Amsterdam Airport Schiphol for analysis. These are described in section 2.2, after the introduction of the technical side of transcribing and related problems in 2.1. Section 3 deals with communication issues, focusing, on the one hand, on the International Civil Aviation Organization (ICAO) and their influence on aviation communication (3.1) and, on the other hand, on the sources and rules necessary for identifying, analyzing and solving transcription problems and typical mistakes (3.2).

2 The "Setting": Technical Devices and Source of Communication

It is not only the actual aviation communication that can cause problems; they can also be rooted in "surrounding" aspects, such as technical devices and characteristics of the place where the communication was recorded. These problems and their consequences for the transcription process are described in the following subchapter.

2.1 Transcription Techniques

There are several forms and techniques to make transcripts, depending on source, software and intended purpose. Typically, "transcription" is the "typing-up of one's own recordings, as automatic speech recognition is impossible when more than one person is involved".[1] As more than one person is involved in aviation communication and a wide range of interferences/static noises occur, it is not possible to use automatic speech recognition (ASR) for transcribing.

2.1.1 Recording

The website LiveATC[2] was used as a resource for aviation communication recordings. It offers the possibility to listen to live Air Traffic Control (ATC) communication all over the world – at least, in countries in which it is officially allowed. To record these live feeds, a stream recorder can be used.[3]

2.1.2 Setting Time Marks and Preparing the Recording for Transcription

To make a proper transcription, a player with some special functions is needed. These functions include the possibility of reduced playback speed, a short interval in which the transmission is automatically rewound for one or two seconds when pressing "stop" and adjustable time intervals to rewind and fast-forward.[4] These programs can typically be used with a foot pedal, which makes it easier to time the events accurately.

After obtaining the recording (now an mp3-file on the computer), the next step in compiling a transcript is to stop the running time of the radio messages so that every sentence of the later transcript can be traced back in the recording. State-of-the-art technology and XML multi-layer representation formats allow the insertion of time codes and offer an easy way to align the words to the time codes (cf. Geoffrois et al. 2000).

2.1.3 Transcription

As mentioned above, ASR cannot be applied because of several reasons (speech rate, number of speakers, noise, etc.). Consequently, the radio transmissions have to be transcribed manually. This is very time consuming, since very often sequences have to be played several times until everything is understood correctly. Sometimes things are misunderstood, simply because of a lack of background knowledge or because of the bad quality of a transcription. Often enough, there are unclear sections, omissions, overlapping speech segments, noise, etc. Unintelligible words should be marked in the same way throughout the whole

---

[1] http://www.audiotranskription.de/english/transcription/how-to-transcribe/tipps.html
[2] http://www.LiveATC.net
[3] e.g. WM Recorder 14 (http://www.wmrecorder.com/)
[4] e.g. f4 (http://www.audiotranskription.de/english/f4.htm) and Express Scribe (http://www.audiotranskription.de/english/transcription/software/expressscribe)

transcription. In the produced transcriptions, indications in square brackets were used. Where possible, the reason (noise, volume) was given as well. For the transcription guidelines we used GAT (cf. Selting et al. 1998).

The problems which arose from the rather "technical" side do, of course, not just affect the transcriber but, in the first place, pilots and air traffic controllers. Most of the time they have the advantage of being very experienced and being used to their way of communication. If, nevertheless, they do not understand something the other one has said, a simple "say again, please" restores mutual understanding. No serious problems occurred in the transcribed samples.

2.2 Airports

We started off with two European airports: Paris-Orly Airport and Amsterdam Airport Schiphol. The transcripts of the communication between ATC and aircraft approaching these airports serve as examples for this chapter. The characteristics of both airports will be given in the following.

2.2.1 Paris-Orly

Paris-Orly Airport (Aéroport de Paris-Orly) was chosen as the busiest airport in terms of French domestic traffic and second busiest airport in France in overall passenger numbers. The interesting aspect of French airports, however, is the fact that two of the languages allowed by the ICAO for civil aviation communication[5] are spoken there: English and French. Apart from the controller's ability to quickly switch back and forth between the two languages, the most interesting aspect is that sometimes both languages are used within one sentence, i.e. that we can find code-switching and code-mixing. Especially common French expressions such as "écoute" or "d'accord" are used in English transmission as well, as the following example shows:

"Écoute, this is three thousand feet, zero one eight."[6]

The distribution between the languages during half an hour of aviation communication at Paris-Orly Approach is displayed in Table 1.

---

[5] The following languages are officially allowed: Arabic, Chinese, English, French, Russian and Spanish (http://www.ivao.aero/rulregs/general.htm).
[6] Paris-Orly Approach, 2010-10-14, 1133 UTC

Spoken Language	Time
French	00:07:20,7
English	00:05:30,5
Mixture of both	00:01:12,4
Total Speaking Time[7]	00:14:30,5

Table 1: Languages used at Paris-Orly Approach (2010-10-14, 1133 UTC)

A possible problem might be that pilots and controllers have to know both the French AND English phraseology and use it the right way. Experienced pilots may well be used to French controllers' sentences beginning with such expressions, but inexperienced pilots or simply non-native speakers may react in a confused manner – or even show no reaction at all as they do not feel that they are being addressed.

Understanding can be inhibited by the occasional strong French accent of the controllers. So even if all transmissions are done in English, a non-native speaker might not understand them (completely) or not identify the transmissions as English ones.

2.2.2 Amsterdam Airport Schiphol

The 5th largest airport in Europe, Amsterdam Airport Schiphol is the main airport in the Netherlands and an important hub for European transport. Even though Dutch is the Netherlands' official language, it is not one of the ICAO's working languages and therefore English is, at least theoretically, used exclusively at the airport. This makes communication much more fluent than at Paris-Orly, for example. Nevertheless, there are always some short conversations in Dutch between Dutch pilots (mainly from the airline KLM) and controllers as well as short expressions, such as those mentioned for the Paris-Orly airport, e.g.:

"Goedenmiddag, KLM two zero Hotel."
"Goedendag, KLM eight eight Bravo, wind one seven zero, one three knots, continue."[8]

These are used by pilots of every mother tongue as a courtesy. But all in all, Dutch is used much less than French at Paris-Orly, as can be seen in Table 2.

---

[7] including fragments and noisy/unintelligible transmissions
[8] Amsterdam Schiphol Approach 2011-11-01, 1146 UTC

Spoken Language	Time
Dutch	00:00:24,5
English[9]	00:17:47,1
Mixture of both	00:00:26,5
Total Speaking Time[10]	00:19:28,7

Table 2: Languages used at Amsterdam Schiphol Approach (2011-11-01, 1146 UTC)

So altogether, English as a working language is much more accepted in Amsterdam, due to the lack of an alternative. For further information on English as a Lingua Franca cf. Hansen-Schirra, this volume.

3 The Content: Communication between Tower and Pilot

Particularities of the "setting" constitute the first (and smaller) part of problems that can appear during the transcription process. A second area, which already figured in the description of the language particularities at the airports, is the actual communication between the tower and the pilot. In order to identify and solve communication problems here, the ICAO documents provide a good source of information.

3.1 ICAO and Regulated Transmission

All of today's regulations, rules and the whole process of aviation communication, as described here, are a result of the ICAO. As ICAO itself states, without its regulations and standards, "our aviation system would be at best chaotic and at worst unsafe".[11] The basic regulations concerning aviation communication they developed are presented and discussed in the following.

3.1.1 Transmission in General

Documents such as the *Manual of Radiotelephony* (ICAO 2007), lay down some basic rules as to how transmissions should be done. Every transmission should be carried out in a "normal conversational tone" with clear and distinct pronunciation. The rate of speech should not exceed 100 words per minute and should be reduced if the message is written down by the recipient. A slight pause is recommended before and after numbers and other important information (call signs,

---

[9] including transmissions with only one Dutch word such as the greeting "goedemorgen" (good morning)
[10] including fragments and noisy/unintelligible transmissions
[11] „Making a Standard", ICAO, http://www.icao.int/icao/en/anb/mais/index.html, accessed 2011-06-11

waypoints). Hesitation sounds ("er", "ehm", etc.) should be avoided and long transmissions should be interrupted by short pauses to make them easier to understand.

3.1.2 Transmission of Letters, Numbers and Digits

As letters, numbers and digits are essential parts of every message, particular attention is paid to their use and pronunciation. In aviation, letters should be spelled according to the NATO spelling alphabet[12], i.e. every letter is replaced by a word that "typically replaces the name of the letter with which it starts (acrophony)".[13] This is not to be confused with a phonetic alphabet, such as the IPA (International Phonetic Alphabet), for example. If correct reception of letters, e.g. in the case of waypoints, is required, the spelling alphabet comes into use. Table 3 shows some examples of waypoints and the corresponding shortcuts in airspace above and around Amsterdam.

Point	Shortcut	Spelling Alphabet
SCHIPHOL	SPL	Sierra Papa Lima
PAMPUS	PAM	Papa Alpha Mike
SPIJKERBOOR	SPY	Sierra Papa Yankee

Table 3: Waypoints

For airlines' call signs, such as KLM (Royal Dutch Airline, Koninklijke Luchtvaart Maatschappij), however, the phonetic alphabet is used (i.e., /keɪ el em/ instead of Kilo Lima Mike).

Distinguishing between the two alphabets and their respective use is important not only for pilots and controllers, but also for the transcriber. In aviation communication, these rules help to make communication unambiguous; not knowing them may lead to wrong transcriptions. Sometimes even pilots or controllers do not apply these rules correctly, resulting in another source for misunderstandings, like in the following example: "ILS approach" (ILS = instrument landing system) was not spelled according to the phonetic alphabet, i.e. /aɪ el es/, but as an acronym, which made the first transcription read "idles approach" instead of "ILS approach".

Digits should be transmitted with a clear pronunciation. Similar-sounding words may be misunderstood because many non-native speakers of English find it difficult to correctly pronounce the voiceless dental fricative "th". Therefore, for

---

[12] "NATO phonetic alphabet: Digits", Wikipedia, http://en.wikipedia.org/wiki/NATO_phonetic_alphabet#Digits, accessed 2011-08-10
[13] http://en.wikipedia.org/wiki/Spelling_alphabet, accessed 2011-08-10

example, "three" is pronounced /tri:/ ("tree") and "thousand" as /'taʊ.zənd/ ("tousand"). Other distinguishing features are the digits "four" and "nine" to which an extra syllable is added ("fower" and "niner"). This way, for instance, the digit "four" cannot be confused with the preposition "for" which might lead to problematic misunderstandings.

In numbers with more than one digit, every digit is pronounced separately – regardless of whether they are part of an airline call sign, a flight level, etc., see Table 4. The decimal point should be transmitted by spelling out the word "decimal".

Point	Shortcut
AZ 2952	ALITALIA two niner five two
FL 180	flight level one zero eight
18 R	runway one eight right

Table 4: Use of digits

3.1.3 Basic Phraseology

The phraseology in aviation communication follows some basic rules and only uses a defined contingent of standard words and phrases. The meaning of every phrase is given by the ICAO and has to be completely unambiguous (see *Table 5* for some examples).

Word/Phrase	Meaning
AFFIRM	Yes.
APPROVED	Permission for proposed action granted.
CLEARED	Authorized to proceed under the conditions specified.
CONFIRM	I request verification of: (*clearance, instruction, action, information*).
NEGATIVE	No. / Permission not granted. / This is not correct. / Not capable.
STANDBY	Wait and I will call you.

Table 5: Phraseology (cf. ICAO 2007)

3.2 Other Sources of Information

While compiling the transcript, it was possible to draw on a variety of different sources of information which help to understand the conversation between controller and pilot. First of all there is the specific phraseology mentioned above. ICAO (2007) provides a broad overview of operating procedures and aerodrome control at an airport and helps to gain an understanding of general aviation phraseology. Further information is given by the comprehensive ICAO 2001 and other official documents published by the ICAO.[14]

While phraseology accounts for about 50 % of total communication, the other 50 % consist of airline call signs, names, way points, other flight information and specifications and some non-phraseological specialist terminology relating to comments or transmissions.

As well as the ICAO information, all this documentation reflects the need in aviation communication for clearly defined rules and very detailed specifications, exemplified in the following two sections on airlines and runways. Only when speaker and listener have this extensive background knowledge, can communication be successful. For a correct transcription of aviation communication, background knowledge is crucial, too.

3.2.1 Airlines

In order to identify abbreviations etc. concerning airlines, standards were developed providing ICAO and IATA[15] codes, the country of origin and the call sign of every airline. *Table 6* displays the entry for the Turkish "Pegasus Airline", for example.

Airline	Country	Call Sign	IATA	ICAO
Pegasus Airlines	Turkey	SUNTURK	PC	PGT

Table 6: Airlines

Not checking the assumed call sign may lead to an amusing transcript such as the following (from Schiphol Airport):

"DELTA FORCE two two niner, one eight center, cleared to land."[16]

Flight number and call sign clearly indicate that the "Delta Air Lines" with the flight number 4229 is meant which should not be confused with "Delta Force" or "Delta for", etc. Here, again, unclear pronunciation and lacking background knowledge can lead to problems in the transcription.

---

[14] http://www2.icao.int/en/home/default.aspx, accessed 2011-09-29
[15] International Air Transport Association
[16] Amsterdam Schiphol Approach 2011-11-01, 1146 UTC

3.2.2 Runways

Other resources are several aerodrome, departure, arrival and runway charts as provided by the Aeronautical Information Service (AIS) Netherlands.[17] The arrival and departure charts display the different way points (e.g. ARTIP near Schiphol) and names of specific travel routes. An overview of the runways and their current orientation is another important source of information. Amsterdam Schiphol airport, for example, has several runways (see *Table 7*).

Nr.	Runway	Orientation
1	Polderbaan	18R/36L
2	Kaagbaan	06/24
3	Buitenveldertbaan	09/27
4	Aalsmeerbaan	18L/36R
5	Zwanenburgbaan	18C/36C
6	Oostbaan	04/22

Table 7: Schiphol runways

The following example shows that controllers tend not to give the specification "runway", e.g.

"Continue approach one eight center, DELTA four two two niner."[18]

Knowing the orientation of the runways makes it possible to infer the correct transcription and thus the orientation: "the Zwanenburgbaan with the orientation 18C/36C".

4 Conclusion

There are many things that can affect aviation communication and lead to more or less serious problems in understanding. Wrong application of communication rules, unclear pronunciation, etc. can result in difficulties for pilots and controllers as well as for those transcribing their communication.

Most of the time, Pilots and controllers can compensate for this lack of understanding because of their experience. Therefore problems in communication only constitute a real danger in very few cases. Nevertheless, as a transcriber, one has to be aware not only of the rules of aviation communication, but also of the fact that these rules are not always applied. Here, extensive background knowledge helps in overcoming the resulting difficulties in understanding.

---

[17] http://www.ais-netherlands.nl/index.html
[18] Amsterdam Schiphol Approach 2011-11-01, 1146 UTC

Wendy Fox is a student at the FTSK in Germersheim and is currently doing her MA in Language, Culture and Translation. She was responsible for the transcriptions in the project "Interferences, conflicts and challenges in high risk communication – an empirical study of international aviation communication".

References

Geoffrois, Edouard/Claude Barras/Steven Bird/Zhibiao Wu (2000): "Transcribing with Annotation Graphs", in *Proceedings of the Second International Conference on Language Resources and Evaluation*, 1517-1521. http://trans.sourceforge.net/articles/Transcriber-LREC2000.ps.gz

ICAO (International Civil Aviation Organization) (2001): *Air Traffic Management*, 14th edition. ICAO Document 4444-ATM/501.

ICAO (International Civil Aviation Organization) (2007): *Manual of Radiotelephony*, 4th edition. ICAO Document 9432-AN/925.

Selting, Margret et al. (1998): "Gesprächsanalytisches Transkriptionssystem (GAT)", in: *Linguistische Berichte* 173, 91-122.

Silja Koble
Patricia Roh

Linguistic Characteristics of Aviation English and their Practical Use – an Analysis

1 Introduction

The *Deutsche Flugsicherung* (DFS) in Germany is responsible for controlling about three million flights per year (cf. DFS 2009: 8). To keep a high safety level, efficient communication between all parties involved in air traffic, especially between pilots and controllers, is very important. In order to achieve uniform and unambiguous flight communication, binding standard guidelines were issued. Thus spoken English used in international flight communication became an artificial and reduced functional variety of the English language. This article will highlight the linguistic characteristics of Aviation English. The practical use of Aviation English was examined within the framework of a linguistic seminar at the Johannes Gutenberg University of Mainz, Faculty of Translation Studies, Linguistics and Cultural Studies in Germersheim. The results of this project will constitute the main part of this article.

2 Basic Principles of Flight Communication

Radio communication used in air traffic follows the rules of a "communication loop" (*Figure 1*).

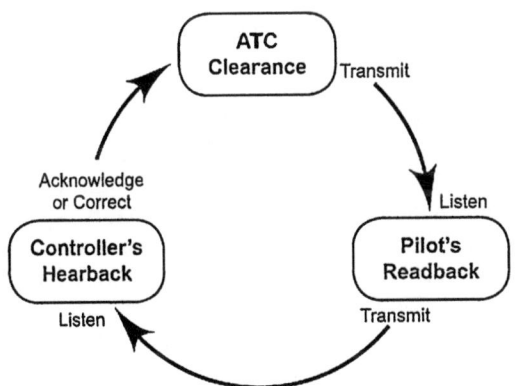

Figure 1: The Pilot-Controller Communication Loop (cf. EUROCONTROL 2006: 23)

The controller transmits his instructions via radio communication, while the pilot listens attentively and repeats the instructions word for word in a so-called readback. In turn, the controller listens attentively to the pilot's readback (= hearback) and confirms or corrects it (cf. Rubenbauer 2009: 66-67). Since flight communication is transmitted orally, it has to be as unambiguous as possible, even under extreme time pressure.

Communication in international air traffic usually takes place in English. Countries with a special language status within the International Civil Aviation Organization (ICAO) are allowed to use their own language for national flight control. Apart from English, the so-called ICAO languages are French, Spanish, Russian, Arabic and Chinese. Pilots and controllers do not only have to be fluent in Aviation English, but also in general English (plain English) in order to adequately handle situations not covered by ICAO standard phraseology. In both pilot and controller professional formation, special emphasis is put on English language proficiency. It was not until 2008 that the ICAO introduced an international standard of English language proficiency for both controllers and pilots. To operate in international air traffic, they have to reach at least level four ("operational") of six of the ICAO Language Proficiency Requirements. This also applies to native speakers of English. They have to speak particularly slowly, without a strong dialect or accent and avoid using idiomatic expressions (cf. Rubenbauer 2009: 29-32).

A strong accent or dialect can have a negative impact on transmission comprehensibility. This is equally important for native English speakers as for those who speak it as a second or foreign language. Further problems may arise as a consequence of a high speech rate and long and complex messages. Especially during phases of high work load, controllers tend to put a lot of information into one single transmission, which significantly reduces the comprehensibility of the message (cf. Cardosi et al. 1998: 23 and Bieswanger this volume). As instructions in flight communication contain a multitude of numbers, it is not surprising that single digits concerning altitude, heading and call signs are sometimes switched accidentally. In a worst case scenario, call sign confusion might lead a pilot to carry out instructions meant for another aircraft. Apart from distraction and fatigue, noise is a factor that might cause misunderstandings in flight communication. Cultural differences as well as code switching, i.e. continuous switching between Aviation English and plain English, can in some cases lead to misunderstandings. Blocked transmissions account for technical difficulties in flight communication, when one transmission is blocked by a transmission sent from another aircraft (cf. Rubenbauer 2009: 11).

All factors mentioned above may lead to readback or hearback errors. Pilot-controller communication is then no longer unambiguous and can cause misinterpretations and misunderstandings. For this reason, it is important for pilots and controllers to speak slowly and clearly, to keep their messages short and concise and to listen to and repeat transmissions attentively.

3 Characteristics of Aviation English

3.1 Grammar

Aviation English is an artificial language based on English grammar and vocabulary. Its syntax is reduced to a minimum; sentences have to be as short and as simply structured as possible. The following grammatical characteristics are typical for Aviation English.

In order to keep sentences simple, few articles, pronouns and auxiliary verbs are used. The use of subjects should be avoided. An exception is the use of a call sign in subject position at the beginning of a phrase, e.g. "Air Canada 452 cleared to land". The use of imperatives like "Say again!" instead of complicated interrogative forms like "Could you please say again?" is common. Pilots use progressive forms to give information on ongoing actions, for example "holding position". However, the use of these forms should be kept to a minimum because of their potential to cause ambiguity. Future tenses are rarely used and if so, only as "will"-constructions (cf. Intemann 2008: 73-74). Prepositions are rarely used. They must be avoided directly before and after numbers, since the homonymy or similarity of "to" and "two", "for" and "four" or "on" and "one", for instance, could cause ambiguity. Instead of "climb to five zero" a pilot might understand "climb two five zero" and ascend to an altitude he has not been cleared to (cf. Cushing 1994: 14). Instructions concerning flight level are always transmitted without prepositions, but with the addition "flight level", as in "climb to flight level five zero" (cf. Rubenbauer 2009: 40).

3.2 Phonetics

In Aviation English, there are also special regulations for the pronunciation of words and numbers, which in some cases deviate from their pronunciation in general English (cf. ICAO 2007: 2-1).

First of all, pilots and controllers have to speak clearly and at a constant volume. The speech rate should be unchanging and should not exceed 100 words per minute. Short breaks before and after numbers help to ease the transmission of numerical information. Fillers like "ah", "uh" and "er" should be avoided. The ICAO Alphabet is used to indicate waypoints and taxiways and to transmit call signs. It is identical with the NATO Alphabet and starts with Alpha, Bravo, Charlie (cf. ICAO 2007: 2-2 and 2-3).

When transmitting numbers, it is important to know that the voiceless dental fricative θ in the term "three" shifts to the voiceless alveolar plosive t. Thus, "three" /θriː/ is pronounced "tree" /triː/. The number "nine" /naɪn/ becomes "niner" /naɪnəʳ/ in order to avoid confusion with the number "five", which is monosyllabic as well (cf. Rubenbauer 2009: 37-38). For the same reasons, the number "four" /fɔːʳ/ is pronounced "fower" /fouəʳ/. Numbers are always given digit by digit. Thus, "245" is spoken "two four five". Only flight level and visibility can be given in hundreds and thousands. The number of hundreds and thousands has to be spoken digit by digit, followed by the term "hundred" or "thousand", e.g. "one two thousand" for "12,000" and "three thousand four hundred" for "3,400". Decimal numbers are also given digit by digit and are separated by the term "decimal", e.g. "one two decimal eight" for "12.8" (cf. ICAO 2007: 2-3 to 2-5).

3.3 Standard Phraseology

ICAO standard phraseology was developed as a consequence of a fatal aircraft crash in Tenerife in 1977, which was caused mainly by ambiguous radio communication. ICAO standard phraseology is a list of terms and phrases designed especially to make flight communication unambiguous and thus safer. ICAO standard phraseology phrases have been carefully determined in order to avoid homonyms and thus possible misunderstandings. Instead of using the term "ascent", "climb" must be used to avoid confusion with the term "descent" (cf. Intemann 2008: 73). Another example is the use of the term "affirm" instead of "affirmative", as the similar word endings of "affirmative" and "negative" could lead to misunderstandings in communication (cf. McMillan 1998: 43). Every term and phrase of ICAO standard phraseology has a precisely defined meaning: "cleared" and "clearance" should only be used in direct relation to the event of take-off. For all other clearances, the terms "approved" and "approval" must be used (cf. Rubenbauer 2009: 61).

All instructions in flight communication follow the same pattern. First of all, an aircraft's call sign has to be given in order to let the pilot know that the following instructions are meant for him. Afterwards, instructions are transmitted by using ICAO standard phraseology. The pilot's readback has to contain his call sign as well, so the controller can identify the sender of the message.

The use of standard phraseology is obligatory for all ICAO member states. In daily flight communication, however, deviations can be found quite often, especially in emergency situations or when complicated information has to be transmitted. In these situations, there is no specific standard phraseology that can be applied. Greetings and polite phrases are also considered to be deviations from standard phraseology and should be avoided, since they are not necessary to transmit information or instructions. On the other hand, they help to make pilot – controller relationships more personal (cf. Rubenbauer 2009: 72). Standard phraseology must be used, especially when transmitting numerical information, in high workload situations or in case of communication problems of any kind. Otherwise, messages might be misinterpreted and the recipient might carry out instructions that were not meant for him.

4 Aviation English Applied

4.1 Analysis Setup

Within the framework of the linguistic seminar "World Englishes" (winter semester 2010/11) at the Johannes Gutenberg University of Mainz, Faculty of Translation Studies, Linguistics and Cultural Studies in Germersheim, the linguistic aspects of Aviation English were examined in detail. Eight transcripts of pilot – controller communication on flights of an American, a Canadian, a Chinese, a Japanese, a German, a Swiss, an Arabic and a Thai airline were analyzed, whereas in-cockpit communication was not looked at. Of the examined transcripts, three can be categorized as emergency situations and five as routine situations. The transcripts include 5,540 words and were analyzed regarding the following linguistic elements: articles, pronouns, auxiliary and modal verbs, prepositions, greetings, polite phrases, colloquial speech, fillers, imperatives, future and progressive forms.

4.2 Analysis Results

The first examined transcript has 984 words and describes a Canadian airline's routine flight. At first, there seems to be a consistent use of standard phraseology. However, some minor deviations can be found, for example the use of "clear" instead of "cleared" for a clearance or the progressive form "requesting" instead of "request". Numbers are often grouped in pairs of two like "eighteen" instead of "one eight". Overall, there are 68 prepositions (6.9 %), of which 29 prepositions are used right before or after numbers. In one sector a lot of plain English is used, thus a lot of articles (1.6 %) and pronouns (1.9 %) can be found. Presumably, this is because both pilot and controller are native speakers of English.

The second transcript consisting of 1,140 words describes an emergency situation involving a Swiss airline. Most deviations from ICAO standard phraseology in this transcript derive from grouping numbers into pairs of two. Since it is an emergency situation, plain English is used with a lot of articles (4.8 %), pronouns (7.0 %), auxiliary verbs (1.2 %), modal verbs (1.1 %) and prepositions (6.5 %). Instead of "affirm", the more colloquial "okay" is used several times. Furthermore, there are a lot of fillers (4.7 %), presumably because the pilot is not a native speaker of English. Although they are in an emergency situation, pilot and controller stay polite (e.g. "May we do that?", "When you have time could I have…"). Despite the pilot presumably being a non-native speaker of English, he effectively switches to plain English. Nevertheless, standard phraseology is mostly applied until the end of the transcript.

The third transcript includes 253 words and describes communication between an American controller and a Chinese pilot, who is obviously not proficient enough in English to make himself understood. Both pilot and controller adhere to ICAO standard phraseology, but while the American controller speaks clearly, the Chinese pilot has a strong accent. As soon as the controller realizes he has not been understood, he switches to plain English and uses very simple phrases like "ramp people" for "Apron Control" or "okay" instead of "affirm". Since communication is now taking place in plain English, a lot of articles (7.1 %), pronouns (7.5 %) and prepositions (7.9 %) can be found. The situation gets complicated when the Chinese pilot misunderstands the controller's question for a clearance, possibly because of an unfamiliar intonation or pitch. Fortunately, since this was a routine situation while taxiing, the miscommunication had no serious consequences. In an emergency situation, the Chinese pilot could not have made himself understood in English. Here, the necessity of the ICAO Language Proficiency standard becomes evident.

In the fourth transcript, the contact between the controller and the pilot of a German airline is lost. The transcript has 998 words. A lot of imperatives (3.5 %) can be found, as well as a great number of prepositions (3.2 %), which are also used before numbers (especially the preposition "on" before "one"). When plain English is employed, a lot of pronouns (3.0 %), articles (1.6 %), prepositions (3.2 %) and fillers (1.8 %) are noticeable. Furthermore, numbers are grouped in pairs of two, and pilot and controller deviate from standard phraseology (e.g. "point" instead of "decimal"). Both pilot and controller leave out parts of the long call sign in order to shorten transmissions. All in all, the transcript shows a balanced mixture of Aviation English and plain English.

The fifth transcript describes a near midair collision of two Japanese aircraft. The pilots adhere to ICAO standard phraseology with only a few exceptions. The controllers only deviate twice by saying "nine" for "niner" and by using a preposition directly after a number. Within the whole transcript, there is only one sentence in plain English, which also contains the only article used. Compared to the overall word count of 792 words, the number of pronouns (1.0 %) and prepositions (1.9 %) is small. Some greetings (0.6 %) and polite phrases (0.4 %) are exchanged, as well as 15 fillers (1.9 %). Of all transcripts examined in this analysis, ICAO standard phraseology is best applied in this fourth transcript. Here, effective communication and focused attention on behalf of the pilots helped to prevent a midair collision.

The sixth transcript has 556 words and describes a go-around situation in the vicinity of an airport. There are only a few deviations from ICAO standard phraseology, e.g. "yes" instead of "affirm" and the preposition "to" before the number "two". Because of landing complications, plain English with a lot of pronouns (2.3 %), prepositions (3.2 %) and polite phrases (1.3 %) prevails. Furthermore, the Thai pilot does not give his call sign several times, and the controller groups several pieces of information into one long transmission instead of giving the instructions in several short transmissions. Overall, this transcript is another balanced mixture of Aviation English and plain English.

In the seventh transcript, ICAO standard phraseology is observed as well. Within 248 words, there are just a few prepositions (2.8 %), of which only one is used directly after a number. The number of pronouns (3.6 %) and articles (0.8 %) is small as well. However, it is noticeable that the pilot of an Arabic airline only gives his call sign four times. Although the aircraft is in an emergency situation and eventually makes a belly landing, the pilot stays calm and explains his situation and his requirements objectively. For instance, he repeats the phrase "Request emergency service" three times. All in all, this transcript shows effective emergency communication.

The eighth and last of the examined transcripts has 569 words and describes the emergency landing of an American airline due to a bird strike. Mostly plain English is used, thus there is a large number of articles (2.8 %), pronouns (9.7 %), auxiliary verbs (1.1 %), modal verbs (1.2 %) and prepositions (4.7 %). Here as well, "okay" is used instead of "affirm". Furthermore, there are a lot of fillers (3.0 %), presumably due to uncertainty or stress. Probably for the same reason, the pilot does not give his call sign in every transmission. Since this is an emergency situation with no applicable standard phraseology, plain English is used most of the time. It is assumed that pilot and controller, both Americans, automatically switch to their mother tongue in an emergency situation.

Table 1 and *Table 2* show the use of the analyzed linguistic elements in all eight transcripts. The three transcripts describing emergency situations are marked with an asterisk behind the country code. The two bottom lines give the total number of each element and their proportion to the overall total of 5,540 words.

Country	Articles	Pronouns	Auxiliary verbs	Modal verbs	Prepositions	Greetings
CDN	16	19	7	2	68	6
CH*	55	80	14	12	74	5
CHN	18	19	6	0	20	0
D	16	30	2	0	32	2
J	1	8	1	0	15	5
T	4	13	4	2	18	2
UAE*	2	9	0	0	7	2
USA*	16	55	6	7	26	0
Σ	128	233	40	23	260	22
%	2.3	4.2	0.7	0.4	4.7	0.4

Table 1: Numbers of all analyzed linguistic elements in eight transcripts, part 1

Country	Polite phrases	Colloquial English	Fillers	Imperatives	Future	Progressive
CDN	3	0	2	31	1	11
CH*	10	11	54	19	9	16
CHN	0	6	6	9	0	0
D	6	2	18	35	1	7
J	3	0	15	36	0	11
T	7	1	0	12	3	8
UAE*	0	0	2	7	1	2
USA*	4	7	17	7	1	5
Σ	33	27	114	156	16	60
%	0.6	0.5	2.1	2.8	0.3	1.1

Table 2: Numbers of all analyzed linguistic elements in eight transcripts, part 2

4.3 Interpretation of Results

The use of articles, pronouns, auxiliary verbs and prepositions was significantly higher in situations where a lot of plain English was used. Modal verbs, especially "can", were used more in emergency situations than in routine situations. In half of the analyzed transcripts, no modal verbs could be found at all. Greetings and polite phrases were used depending on the situation, especially in frequency changes. Colloquial English was used in transmissions in plain English in order to facilitate communication with non-native speakers of English and in emergency situations. Fillers were used in emergency situations, presumably because of uncertainty and stress in the cockpit. Imperatives can be found very often, since they are a characteristic element of Aviation English. The number of imperatives in each transcript complies with the average value in all transcripts combined. Future forms were the least applied element (0.3 %). Progressive forms were only used by pilots to give descriptions of ongoing actions. The number of progressive forms in each transcript differs only slightly from the average value in all transcripts combined.

The analysis of eight transcripts showed that plain English with a lot of articles, pronouns, prepositions and auxiliary verbs was mostly used in non-routine and emergency situations. Only in one case the respective pilot remained calm and adhered to ICAO standard phraseology in an emergency situation. One transcript showed many deviations from ICAO standard phraseology. The respective Chinese pilot was a non-native speaker of English, who seemed to have an insufficient command of both Aviation English and plain English. In one transcript, ICAO standard phraseology was used consistently and with only minor deviations.

5 Outlook

Since the introduction of ICAO standard phraseology, and especially in the past few years, flight communication has improved considerably. Obligatory regulations and standardizations have made Aviation English increasingly unambiguous and thus more efficient. Numerous scientific analyses about communication problems in Aviation English have contributed to this. The present analysis is focused on the linguistic characteristics of Aviation English. It shows that both pilots and controllers deviate from ICAO standard phraseology, even in routine situations. Furthermore it became evident that English language proficiency is crucial in order to communicate efficiently in emergency situations. Of course, communication problems do not necessarily lead to incidents or accidents. However, further improvements in security could be achieved, for instance by raising awareness of linguistic communication problems in pilot and controller formation, by training to understand different accents and by applying further controls of compliance with ICAO standard phraseology (cf. McMillan 1998: 47; Intemann 2008: 86).

Another possible improvement could be the introduction of a visual communication system to fully or partially replace spoken pilot – controller communication. Such a system would evade all problems deriving from spoken transmissions, e.g. a strong accent or a high speech rate. Being a readable system, it would be unambiguous and reduce misunderstandings. A similar system that is already in use today is CPDLC (Controller Pilot Data Link Communications), commonly named Data Link. This system is obligatory for all European aircraft and is primarily used in cruise flight.

Silja Koble graduated in Business Administration, Tourism and Travel Management from Worms University of Applied Sciences, specializing in aviation management. She is currently studying Applied Linguistics, Cultural Studies and Translation (M.A.) for Italian and English at the Faculty of Translation Studies, Linguistics and Cultural Studies *(FTSK) of the University of Mainz in Germersheim. Being passionate about flying, she also works as a flight attendant.*

Patricia Roh studied Applied Linguistics, Cultural Studies and Translation (M.A.) for English and French at the Faculty of Translation Studies, Linguistics and Cultural Studies *(FTSK) of the University of Mainz in Germersheim, specializing in technical and medical translations. She graduated in 2011 and now works as a technical translator and proofreader.*

References

Cardosi, Kim M. / Paul Falzarano / Sherwin Han (1998): *Pilot-Controller Communication Errors: An Analysis of Aviation Safety Reporting System (ASRS) Reports*. Washington, DC: U.S. Department of Transportation, FAA Federal Aviation Administration, Office of Aviation Research (NTIS No. DOT/FAA/AR-98/17).

Cushing, Steven (1994): *Fatal Words: Communication Clashes and Aircraft Crashes*. Chicago: The University of Chicago Press.

DFS Deutsche Flugsicherung (2009): *Luftverkehr in Deutschland. Mobilitätsbericht 2009*. Langen: DFS.

EUROCONTROL (The European Organisation for the Safety of Air Navigation) (2006): *AGC European Action Plan for Air Ground Communications Safety*, edition 1.0. Brussels: EUROCONTROL.

ICAO (International Civil Aviation Organization) (2007): *Manual of Radiotelephony*, 4th edition. ICAO Document 9432-AN/925.

Intemann, Frauke (2008): "'Taipei Ground, Confirm Your Last Transmission Was in English...?' – An Analysis of Aviation English as a World Language", in: Gnutzmann, Claus / Frauke Intemann (ed.): *The Globalisation of English and the English Language Classroom*. 2nd edition. Tübingen: Narr, 71-88.

McMillan, David (1998): *"...Say again?..." Miscommunications in Air Traffic Control*. Brisbane: Queensland University of Technology.

Rubenbauer, Franz (2009): *Linguistics and Flight Safety: Aspects of Oral English Communication in Aviation*. Aachen: Shaker.

César Eugène Holzem

So Much to Say, so Few Words
–
Why Pilots Deviate from Standard Phraseology

1 Introduction

Much can be said about *to what extent* and *how* pilots deviate from the ICAO standard phraseology in aviation communication, as is done in other contributions to this volume. In the following, I will try to provide explanations as to *why* pilots deviate from this standard language – especially when they are not supposed to do so. Several reasons can be identified, of which five will be discussed as the main motives behind deviation, before moving on to the question how they can be dealt with and how communication can be improved.

2 Crew Resource Management

Questions of aviation communication and the problems arising in this context can be discussed in the broader framework of Crew Resource Management (CRM). This section contains a short summary about CRM's main issues and its importance for aviation.

2.1 CRM – What is It About?

Research into aviation accidents at the end of the 1970s revealed that "the primary cause of the majority of aviation accidents was human error, and that the main problems were failures of interpersonal communication, leadership, and decision making in the cockpit".[1] In this context, CRM was introduced as a means of improving interpersonal and situational behavior among the crew as well as between aircraft and air traffic control. It does not focus very much on the crew's knowledge or their ability to operate an aircraft, but rather on mental processes and interpersonal skills, of which communication is one key element. As a first definition, CRM is about understanding *human factors* and *human performance issues* in aviation and managing them in a way that is appropriate to the flight crew's and cabin crew's function while operating an aircraft. In this definition, 'human factors' involve principles which apply to aeronautical design, certification, training, operations and maintenance and which seek a safe interplay between the human and other system components with a proper consideration of human performance.

---

[1] http://www.crewresourcemanagement.net/ (11.8.2011)

'Human performance', on the other hand, refers to human capabilities and limitations which have an impact on the safety and efficiency of aeronautical operations. Besides knowledge and training, here, the focus lies on human behavior. Management of human factors and human performance provides the necessary awareness of these human capabilities and limitations. Moreover, it provides countermeasures to overcome problems resulting from transgression (inadvertent or deliberate) of aviation communication rules. Thus, CRM can be "defined as a management system which makes optimum use of all available resources – equipment, procedures and people – to promote safety and enhance the efficiency of flight operations" (CAA 2006: 1).

Although in its beginning and implementation some 30 years ago it was met with strong reservations, CRM today is one of the main pillars of airline crew training and probably the keystone of non-technical skills training.

It covers – to name only a few – subjects like

- human information processing, attention and perception and situational awareness,
- social psychology issues like motivation and de-motivation, peer pressure and team work,
- management issues in supervision and leadership,
- stress and time pressure, fatigue, workload management,
- and, last but not least, communication issues.

It is important to understand that CRM is not about re-education of flight and cabin crews or about forcing them to adapt their habits. Human performance is not only flawed; human performance also bears the ability to actively contribute to the enhancement of safety in normal and critical situations. Therefore, CRM addresses not only the weaknesses in human performance but also its strength. CRM refers to human performance as an indifferent factor, not a malignant failure. It can be either deteriorating or consolidating.

2.2 CRM – Why do We Need It?

There is a good reason why CRM has reached such an important and exposed position. Although modern aircraft become technically more and more reliable, the number of accidents is still stagnating. In the old days of flying, the likelihood of experiencing engine failure, for example, was such that every pilot had to be prepared to go through this at least once, maybe twice in his professional lifetime. Today it is rather unlikely that a pilot will experience engine failure in his flying career at all. In fact, 80 % of the accidents that are counted today relate solely or primarily to human factors.

Let us take a short look at the total number of aviation accidents, ordered by region (see *Table 1*).

	2009	2008
Africa	14	7
Asia-Pacific	15	19
Commonwealth of Independent States	2	10
Europe	17	17
Latin America & The Caribbean	10	19
Middle East & North Africa	15	12
North America	14	24
North Asia	3	1

Table 1: Total accidents by region (all aircraft types, Eastern and Western-built)

This table shows that accidents occur with similar frequencies in all regions of the world – the region does not seem to have an effect on the overall frequency of accidents. As this table depicts the absolute numbers of accidents, regions with low data do not indicate a safer operational standard. The numbers are low because the total traffic emergence is low, too. A different picture arises when we take the relative rate of *hull loss accidents* into account (see *Table 2*). A hull loss accident is "an aviation accident where the damage to the aircraft is such that it must be written off, or in which the aircraft is totally destroyed".[2] The data here take into account the number of accidents in relation to total traffic emergence. It shows the accident rate per 1 million flight sectors and hence comes to a relative comparability between regions.

Table 2 shows that regions where CRM is well established (e.g. Europe, North America) exhibit significantly fewer hull losses relative to traffic emergence than other regions. It reveals that regions where the absolute number of accidents is comparably low (see *Table 1*, i.e. Africa, C.I.S.) show a high accident rate.[3]

---

[2] http://en.wiktionary.org/wiki/hull-loss_accident (11.8.2011)
[3] Additionally it is important to know that *Table 1* refers to accidents involving aircraft from all manufacturing countries while *Table 2* only collects western-built aircraft types. This is the reason why regions that traditionally use non-western-built airplanes (C.I.S., North Asia = basically P.R. China) show low or no accident rates in *Table 2*. For instance, in 2009 C.I.S. reported 2 and North Asia 3 overall accidents but the western-built hull loss rate in the same year was 0.00 in both regions. This indicates that none of

When examining the regions with low accident rates a valid conclusion is that figures are especially low in areas where CRM has a long tradition and is an accepted integral part of airline crew training. Hence the figures show that the importance of CRM and its further development cannot be denied.

	2005	2006	2007	2008	2009
Africa	9.21	4.31	4.09	2.12	9.94
Asia / Pacific	1.00	0.67	2.76	0.58	0.86
Commonwealth of Independent States	0.00	8.60	0.00	6.43	0.00
Europe	0.33	0.32	0.29	0.42	0.45
Latin America & the Caribbean	2.59	1.80	1.61	2.55	0.00
Middle East & North Africa	3.84	0.00	1.08	1.89	3.32
North America	0.19	0.49	0.09	0.58	0.41
North Asia	0.00	0.00	0.88	0.00	0.00
Industry	0.76	0.65	0.75	0.81	0.71
IATA Member Airlines	0.35	0.48	0.68	0.52	0.62

Table 2: Western-built jet Hull Losses per million sectors 2005-2009[4]

As for German airlines, I will use TUIfly as an example. Here, CRM has a long tradition; it was the first airline in Germany and one of the first in Europe, too, which successfully developed and conducted a joint CRM/TRM course together with DFS Munich Centre in 2007. This course covered overlapping human factors and human performance aspects for both pilots and controllers in one common training program and looked at crucial points in the interface between pilots and controllers. One of these crucial points was identified as being communication.

3 Causes of Deviation in Communication

After this short introduction, let me now come to my main topic, the question why pilots deviate from standard phraseology as set up by ICAO.[5] Obviously,

---

[4] the aircraft involved in the absolute accident data for those regions were of western design. A coarse estimate of the hull loss rate for C.I.S. in 2009 **including** eastern-built types – under the premise that the total sectors remained the same as in 2008 – was 1.29; although this figure is just an approximation it is generally coherent with the empiric data and again supports the thesis that CRM training measurably impacts flight safety as this figure is still far above the safety performance of Europe and North America.
http://www.iata.org/pressroom/pr/Documents/2009AviationSafetyPerformance.pdf (11.8.2011)

[5] http://www.icao.int/ (11.8.2011)

they do not do so just for fun or because they are mean by nature; it is part of human nature to do things of which you know that you should not do them or should do them in a different way. Instead, five reasons can be identified which, in my opinion, provide good explanations as to why pilots still deviate from the standard language. These reasons do not claim to be universally valid or to result from extensive scientific research. They derive mainly from my own (limited) experience, and the (subjective, but careful) observations I made with my specialist knowledge as a CRM Instructor.[6]

In the guidelines on CRM training, several skills are mentioned that are "needed to manage the flight within an organized aviation system" (CAA 2006: 1). These include *cognitive skills* (situational awareness, planning and decision-making) and *interpersonal skills* (communications, teamwork). They refer to what I called *human performance issues* above (see 2.1). The five reasons I identified are all linked to the skill of communication; additionally, one relates to situational awareness (*distraction*), one to teamwork (*oversimplification*), and two to planning and decision making (*justification, deception*).

According to CAA 2006, human performance can be affected by the following factors (cf. CAA 2006: 4 f.): emotional climate, stress, pressure, fatigue, and incapacitation. Stress and pressure figure in most of the five reasons mentioned below, but also fatigue (*distraction*), emotional climate (*justification, deception*), and, at least to some extent, incapacitation (*overcompliance*) are reflected.

3.1 Distraction

Probably the most severe deviation from standard communication is not to communicate at all. This is usually referred to as lost communication or Lost Comm, as it is abbreviated in the aeronautical vocabulary, a vocabulary that is notorious for its addiction to acronyms. And, unfortunately, Lost Comm happens quite regularly, most of the time because flight crew members are distracted.

This is a universal problem, represented for example by information issued by Maastricht Area Control Center; Maastricht ACC is the only Pan-European air traffic control organization controlling the Benelux, the English Channel and North Sea and parts of north-western Germany, an area of high traffic density that conducts up to ¼ of the total air traffic over continental Europe. In the juris-

---

[6] At this point I would like to stress that I do not blame pilots for their non-compliance with the ICAO standard. I neither judge them nor claim for myself that this could never happen to me. Most if not all of these behaviors mentioned further on I could observe on myself. The following explanations are therefore meant in purely descriptive and not in a morally convicting manner.

diction of just this ATC unit, 160 occurrences of Lost Comm were reported in 2004. Further information given by the DFS Deutsche Flugsicherung, the German air traffic control authority that controls the total – commercial and recreational – air traffic over Germany reported 341 cases of lost communication in 2005 in its jurisdiction – and these were only those occurrences when communication was lost for a period of more (!) than 30 minutes.

An important aspect here is cockpit environment. The environmental and situational conditions on the flight deck that contribute to these distractions have been extensively researched and described in CRM literature. However, sometimes a less clinical insight can give a more concise understanding of the issue. A vivid picture of the working environment in a cockpit is drawn in a profane paperback called "The Bluffer's Guide to the Flight Deck" (Beere 2005). This book approaches the aviation world with the earthly and sometimes ironic view of an experienced British flight captain.

It describes the surroundings on the flight deck as follows: imagine yourself locked in the wall closet, with a desk lamp shining right into your face (imitating the low early morning sun on an eastbound flight), and your vacuum cleaner turned on (resembling the noises of the airflow and the air condition system) as well as your radio being tuned into some boring conversation program. Now try to listen to it closely for the next 12 hours but to only occasionally pick up some peculiar phrase that addresses you especially (like the individual ATC clearances for your flight).

Although this description might seem slightly exaggerated, it gives you quite a good impression of the level of pressure and distraction in a cockpit. It is a situation, which would be located in the area marked "hypostress" and "hyperstress" in the Yerkes-Dodson stress curve (see *Figure 1* and cf. Yerkes/Dodson 1908). This curve depicts the development of human performance under pressure.

Here the cognitive skill of *situational awareness* comes into play. It is defined in CAA as the "conscious recognition of all the factors and conditions – operational, technical and human – which affect the safe operation of an aircraft" (CAA 2006: 2). Excessive or too low demands (as depicted in *Figure 1*) can both lead to stress and fatigue and thus negatively influence the pilot's performance.

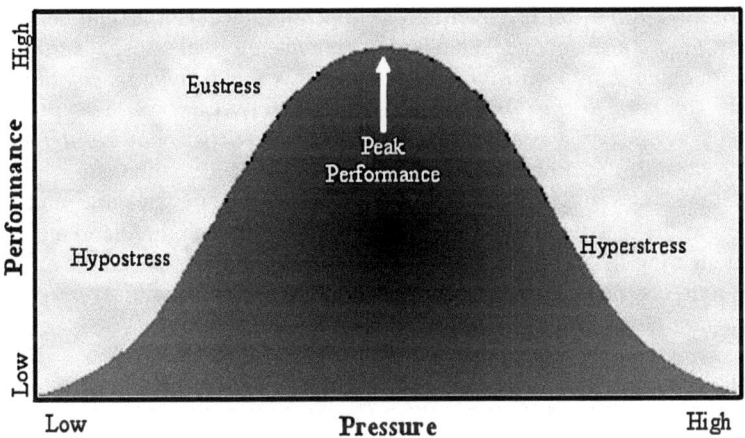

Figure 1: Yerkes-Dodson stress curve[7]

The notable conclusion of this research is that human performance does not only deteriorate under high pressure, which leads to a feeling of being over-challenged, which in turn affects mental alertness. It is also impaired by a low or absent stimulus that results in sub-challenge. Over-challenge occurs in situations in which multiple tasks have to be completed simultaneously to the ongoing radiotelephony. Here, workloads like setting up the aircraft for an approach in a high density air traffic environment, changing these settings on short notice and under time pressure, carefully plotting the aircraft position in difficult terrain, manually controlling the flight path in adverse weather or working on an emergency or abnormal situation in the flight deck interfere with the communication routine. Under this amount of stress, communication is flawed by distraction or preoccupation from non-routine workload. There are examples of pilots in emergency situations who do not communicate with their actual radio call sign anymore (which usually is the airline name followed by the actual flight number) but unintentionally and unperceived switch to some artificial call sign that is used for facilitation only in emergency training in the simulator (like "Flight One-Two-Three"). Once communication behavior is impaired standard phraseology is inadvertently no longer maintained.

We have seen this in another contribution to this volume. In the near miss incident at New York's JFK airport from 2010, in which a South American aircraft almost landed on the wrong runway where another aircraft had just lined up, the

---

[7] http://www.visionjuice.com/resources/shorts/stresscurve.png

air traffic controller, on discovering the impending accident and in audible excitement, mostly abandoned standard communication phrases: "*Aerogal 700 heavy, go around, fly runway heading because you are lining up for the wrong runway. You need to start an immediate right turn [...] But you need to start an immediate right turn, you need to turn right, there's somebody rolling beneath you.*" Again this example shows both flipsides of deviation from standard phraseology. The audible agitation of the speaker underlines the emergency situation to the listener and the urgency for action, on the other hand a clear and distinct steering instruction cannot be read from this communication; in fact the instructions contradict each other in the very same transmission ("*...fly runway [...] start an immediate right turn*").

In contrast to this extreme example, sub-challenge is probably the more common cause for distraction and especially Lost Comm. Ironically, in situations with low workload the communication vigilance also decreases. The absence of stimuli lulls the pilot's alertness below a threshold for constant vigilance. The reason is that the cruise workload, especially in today's highly automated aircraft, is significantly lower than during climb and descent flight phases. Coherent to this are the Maastricht ACC figures mentioned above, as this air traffic control unit conducts an above average portion of cruise traffic. The relatively small Maastricht ACC area of jurisdiction is a major intersection for transcontinental east-west and continental north to south traffic.

A third reason related to the discussed issue is confusion. Often enough pilots do not overhear ATC transmissions because of distraction but also because of confusion. This means that they actively listen to radiotelephony and pick up all or most of the transmissions; however, they overhear a certain address because they do not reassemble the transmission on a cognitive level. Air traffic communication usually addresses an aircraft by its call sign which again usually consists of a combination of the airline name and the flight number (e.g. TUIJet 414, a service from Düsseldorf to Antalya/Turkey). Confusion can occur between same flight numbers with different airlines (e.g. with Lufthansa 414, a service from Munich to Washington D.C.) or similar flight numbers within the same airline operator (e.g. Lufthansa 441, 411 and 421 are parallel services from Houston, New York and Washington to Frankfurt). To prevent this kind of call sign confusion, IATA prohibited airlines from organizing their flight numbers used in radiotelephony with the first digit representing the current weekday a long time ago. This was done because in the afore mentioned case Monday was full of one-... call signs, Tuesdays of two-... call signs and so on. However, this applied countermeasure showed only little benefit. Airlines soon shifted to an organization by world region (like Lufthansa uses 4 for all North American destinations) and debased this idea again – at least within their own operation (inter-airline confusion is often incidentally avoided because the number for each region is randomly chosen, for instance Air France allocate 3 to all North America routes).

A recent strategy to avoid call sign confusion was the introduction of alphanumeric call signs composing a combination of numbers and letters from the ICAO phonetic alphabet (e.g. TUIJet 6PW or 73G, spoken six-Papa-Whiskey or seven-three-Golf, a service from Düsseldorf to Palma de Mallorca and back). Again the benefit of this call sign composition was soon annulled as all the airlines introduced alphanumeric call signs and now the air is once again full of potential confusion as Lufthansa One-Echo-Papa meets TUIJet One-Echo-Papa.

3.2 Oversimplification

Pilots – as well as controllers – often tend to simplify the ICAO standard, ending in oversimplification, a situation where the precautions standard phraseology intended to establish become useless. Examples are:

- Leaving out the reference designations like *heading, runway, flight level, meter or feet, altitude, speed, knots*
- Shortening the values like *90* (nine-zero) instead of *090* (zero-nine-zero); this indication can cause problems when radio communication is deteriorated by the quality of the radio equipment or the environmental conditions (for example: disturbances by solar flares or the use of decameter/HF band frequencies). In situations when the aircraft descends from a high altitude e.g. from Flight Level 340 (i.e. 34.000 ft. in standard atmospheric conditions) to Flight Level 90. Leaving out the prefix 0 prior to 90 can make it difficult to clearly distinguish the cleared flight level from other reasonable altitudes like 190 or 290. Here misunderstanding and confusion are preprogrammed.
- Heading of 040 degrees (of the compass card covering 360 degrees) that is only addressed as four-zero can be misunderstood or confused for 140, 240 or 340.
- A multiplication of these errors can occur when descend and heading information are simultaneously issued by the air traffic controller: a simple but abbreviated clearance like "turn left five-zero, descend eight-zero" bears multiple misunderstandings as both the prefix numbers and the designators are missing and can be easily mistaken for everything from heading 180 to flight level 250 or anything between it and vice versa. To avoid this potential ambiguity standard phraseology calls for this clearance to be read: "turn left heading zero-five-zero degrees, descend flight level zero-eight-zero"; here the double designator "heading" and its dimension unit "degrees" distinguish the heading information from the descend clear-

ance because the dimension unit cannot be reasonably used there and the prefix zero avoids confusion with other possible altitudes or headings that end with 50 or 80. In addition a further avoidance strategy recommends reading only one part of the clearance at a time and waiting for its confirmation before issuing the second part.

These examples do not imply that pilots (or air traffic controllers) are lazy or reckless, but oversimplification occurs because the speaker assumes that his counterpart knows what his abbreviated account means in full standard, i.e. he assumes both communication partners have a common understanding. In fact, most of the time these simplifications are not misleading and the listener understands them correctly. From a time rational point of view those simplifications help to enhance the use of airspace and ATC capacities, especially in dense air traffic environments. From this perspective it is a necessary and active contribution in the area of conflict between thoroughness and effectiveness, an area of conflict that appears when the necessities of the real world meet (or sometimes collide with) the requirements of aseptic ideal conceptions. Still, acceptable simplifications can turn to unacceptable oversimplification and become misleading or ambiguous.

The problem here is where to draw the boundary line: which communication simplifies the standard wording in an acceptable and understandable way, and where is it oversimplified and thus can lead to a potentially dangerous misunderstanding? There is no easy distinction of whether variation of the standard language is acceptable or not. Such a judgment depends on the situation, the participants in the communication process, and many other factors. The single pilot's and controller's personal opinion offers only a subjective boundary and is hence unsuitable for deciding. Here the modern CRM understanding of human performance comes into play: simplification in communication is not a maleficent human failure per se. Its careful application is indifferent. In this area of conflict, Crew Resource Management encourages the crew member to constantly monitor and assess the individual communicational behavior in order to determine a critical convergence to the mentioned boundary line or its undesirable transgression. As CRM does regard the crew member as an active safety stakeholder, the training goal is that whenever simplification is deemed critical, falling back to ICAO communication standard is an effective escape strategy from a maceration of safety. Re-applying this standard does not prove that the pilot did wrong before. Re-applying it proves that the pilot (or controller) actively recovers control of the situation before a hazardous transgression occurs or to re-establish a safe standard.

A first guideline to identify the boundary line is a saying, which is probably also taught in Air Traffic Control Officer (ATCO) training and which can be used here as an apt summary: never base control on assumptions!

3.3 Justification

The ICAO Standard Phraseology was set up for standard situations and to steer an aircraft by Air Traffic Control (ATC). It does not leave room for any additional communication or exhaustive explanations. Nevertheless, there sometimes is a need for more communication, since modern aviation is no longer just the steering of the aircraft (as a manual skill), but the complex organization and management of a flight under many (external) requirements such as economy and efficiency, punctuality and following the schedule, passenger comfort (the last is of course not a primary concern on a cargo aircraft), etc.

Thus, pilots not only want to ask for certain things, such as, in most cases, shortcuts (i.e., the direct way between the departure or an enroute point to the destination) and preferableness (i.e., the request to alter the intended sequencing lay out by the air traffic controller to conduct the traffic and maintain safe distance between the aircraft) – from the ATCO, but also want to support their requests by legitimatizing them with a good and plausible reason. They often do so by using the phrase "request priority" – from a certain point of view this often non-standard wording has become a kind of standard deviation. While it is obvious that the pilot of a delayed flight wants his flight to be prioritized in the controller's sequencing, this phrase is – however widely used and heard across the world – not standard phraseology and cannot be found in the ICAO documents for aeronautical communication.

Other factors which influence communication might be pressure and emotional climate, i.e. "the way that people in the team feel about themselves and each other during flight operations" (CAA 2006: 4). A high level of pressure and a feeling of insecurity might also lead to additional requests and deviations.

Again, we have seen this before in the 2010 case of the South American Aerogal 700 flight approaching the wrong runway at New York's JFK Airport. The Air Traffic Controller, in his excitement not only issued instructions to the crew of this flight to steer the aircraft away from a dangerous encounter with the departing traffic. In his excitement he also underlined the urgency of the situation by adding reasons and justifications for his intervention in colloquial language: *"Aerogal 700 heavy, go around [...] because you are lining up for the wrong runway. [...] But you need to start an immediate right turn [...], there's somebody rolling beneath you."* In this peculiar case, the deviation from standard phraseology probably must be considered a necessary and helpful measure.

Although none of the justification is part of standard phraseology, these additional pieces of information probably helped the pilots to understand the imminent danger and to complete their mental picture of the situation. This mental picture then included the before unseen danger and supported the immediate and forceful execution of the missed approach and the turn away from the runway.

In this context of emotional stress and pressure the speaker sometimes uses non-standard wording to subliminally address a deeper problem. Here, the deviation from standard phraseology is only skin deep. Beneath this deviation the speaker wants to transmit a subliminal message of which he thinks (or hopes) that his counterpart may recognize the requested "priority" as an urgency situation of a more severe kind but the speaker wants to avoid naming this publically on the radio frequency. There are reported cases when aircraft in an urgency or even emergency situations referred to their danger by just using the non-standard phrase "request priority" instead of using standard phraseology for such situations. The ICAO communication rules offer and moreover dictate special wording for those situations. Whenever there is a potential or imminent threat to an aircraft or its passengers the standard wording for an urgency is three repetitions of PAN PAN and for an emergency three repetitions of the famous MAYDAY.[8] However, even in situations where these premises are met pilots often enough refrain from using this standard phraseology. Unfortunately, since the speaker only assumes that his counterpart understands this sub-message the listener does not automatically pick up the message in the way the speaker intended it to be because the meaning of the phrase is not conjointly predefined on an established basis as is the case for all standard phraseology. This can end in nonobservance of the speaker's intention or confusion about the situation. Ironically, both situations are contrary to the speaker's intention of subliminally underlining urgency. I witnessed a case where pilots of another aircraft that was flying just ahead of my flight repeatedly requested "priority" with the air traffic controller over a considerable period of time. The controller first replied that he will see what he can do, upon the fourth repeat he (audibly angry) advised that approach into Frankfurt (the flight was bound for this airport, too) was already restricted and that he was unable to grant any priority; instead the flight should

---

[8] http://en.wikipedia.org/wiki/Pan-pan (25.09.2011): "In radiotelephone communications, a call of three repetitions of PAN-PAN is used to signify that there is an urgency on board a boat, a ship, an aircraft or other vehicle but that, for the time being at least, there is no immediate danger to anyone's life or to the vessel itself. This is referred to as a state of urgency. This is distinct from a MAYDAY call, which means that there is imminent danger to life or to the continued viability of the vessel itself. Thus 'pan-pan' informs potential rescuers (including emergency services and other craft in the area) that a safety problem exists whereas 'Mayday' will call upon them to drop all other activities and immediately initiate a rescue attempt."

prepare to significantly reduce airspeed soon. It was then that the aircraft repeated its request but this time with the phrase "request medical priority". Here it became clear to every listener that the reason for the requested priority was more than just something trivial like punctuality, as it probably was firstly understood. The reason was revealed to be something serious like the medical condition of (probably) one of the passengers. Although the crew obviously considered this condition serious enough to not conduct further flight in the normal air traffic sequence, they did not refer to standard phraseology that was applicable and established for this kind of urgency or maybe even emergency.

3.4 Deception

It may sound strange that pilots sometimes "deceive" their colleagues in the tower by veiling their intentions but this can happen in cases of urgency or emergency. As said before, for declaring urgency (URG) or emergency (EMER), there has to be a situation of imminent danger; assistance will be given as quickly as possible. In the ICAO Standard such situations would be signaled by the PAN PAN or the MAYDAY call. Even though there are clear regulations, guidelines, and formulations for an emergency (checklists, standard phraseology), a deviation from the standard phraseology often occurs by simply using the colloquial *request priority*. Here the speaker wants to avoid a revelation of the urgency or emergency situation. There are several reasons for this deviation:

- Publicity: The pilot does not want to communicate an emergency, because he fears that the tabloids are listening to the aviation communication and will pick up his call – s/he is in a dilemma of high pressure and stress, not only because of the emergency, but also because s/he has to decide whether to run the risk of (maybe unnecessarily) alarming the press or of cutting off quick and adequate help. In fact, the misconception still comes across that an emergency transmission may also alarm the press and that it will lead to adverse headlines for the airline; therefore "letting down the pants" about the nature of a situation should be avoided as long as it is practical; this includes holding back all standard phraseology that can identify the situation – a remarkably odd inversion of the original purpose of standard phraseology.
- "Macho attitude": it sometimes also occurs that pilots simply ignore emergency-like situations and are convinced that as long as they can fly the aircraft there is no real emergency. Here, the factor "emotional climate" comes into play, in the sense of overestimating oneself. This human factor is no longer a passive and complacent behavior but an active and deliberate action that openly conflicts a contribution to safety. However one must add that these cases are rare and exceptional.

- Fear of consequences: This probably is the most comprehensive reason for deception. An emergency call always means drawing special attention to the situation or the caller himself. Ironically again this is the first and pure purpose of an emergency call. However, the actor experiences this also as degradation and fears the consequences that are associated with his emergency call. He is either afraid that an emergency call will provoke further but maybe unnecessary actions by rescue forces or that his perception of the situation is – in retrospect – not shared by others, like air traffic control staff, authorities, the airline company or pilot peers. Both are human and common concerns that derive from social and peer pressure. Both have to do with a subconscious fear of degradation and disgrace.
- A second issue that comes into play here has to do with the fear of failure. Generally, since in all industrial societies the whole educational socialization of the individual is traditionally based on failure as a negative criterion, the fear of failure and a tendency to avoid this kind of negative attention is deeply rooted. Here, CRM training tries to shift the current paradigm of failure away from this traditional understanding as an accusable wrongdoing as it can lead to false retention. Failure is firstly understood as a normal by-product of human performance. Consequently, most airlines that actively support CRM have established non-punitive policies to deal with (unintended) failures of their crews. However this fear still plays an important and, often enough, debilitating role in the individual decision-making process. It is driven by the exposure that the decision will retrospectively be questioned or even judged as being inappropriate, especially by authorities. In this conjunction, when declaring emergency, the fear of generating a false alarm comes to the fore. While on the one hand this retention also proves a responsible handling of the safety resources that will be called to action once emergency is declared, it can on the other hand turn into over-reluctance in a manner that the resources of the rescue chain are spared, even beyond the point where its demand is not only preferable but necessary. Coincidentally the reluctance to make full use of the emergency call is again bred by arguable but insistent myths that circle in the pilot community. Culturally these rumors can be categorized as the aviation equivalent of urban legends (like the famous "tarantula-in-the-window-sill-cactus" story or other modern myths that are usually told as coming from "a friend of a friend"[9]). In fact, it is a common misconception among pilots that once the MAYDAY call is radioed, Air Traffic Control will immediately start off the whole rescue chain: closing runway operations for all other traffic, alerting the fire brigade, informing all hospitals in the

---

[9] For more information cf.: http://en.wikipedia.org/wiki/Urban_legend (27.09.2011)

area, etc. I personally nickname this legend "The Buzzer" as it implies that there is a gigantic red button in the ATC tower that will be pressed immediately when a MAYDAY call is received and virtually unleashes all rescue forces. As urban legends often serve as a modification of cautionary tales (like the famous Fidgety Philip[10]) which should warn the hearer about the consequences of carelessness or recklessness, this particular misconception deepens the reluctance to declare an emergency in order to avoid a false alarm. This legend was finally unmasked in the joint CRM/TRM training between TUIfly pilots and DFS air traffic controllers when the participants from the pilot side repeatedly asked their controller colleagues whether those believed consequences are really associated with a declared emergency or not. They are not: although there is a central emergency button that links an alarm to the airport fire brigade station it is only used for actual or impending crash landings. A MAYDAY call as such usually does not result in alarming the rescue chain. Air traffic controllers will first try to gather as much information as possible about the nature of the emergency to appropriately adjust the rescue measures to the concrete threat.

3.5 Over-Compliance

My last point concerns a cultural issue. Sometimes pilots, especially from the non-English speaking world, tend to over-pronounce phrases, abbreviations, etc. and try to mimic a native accent and language skill. As the aviation world, like many other businesses, set up English as the primary and universal language of international communication, non-native speakers want to avoid giving the impression that they are less able to participate in the business because of language deficiencies. Language skills underline the professional self conceptions of the speaker and are used as a noticeable identification of professionalism. And the conception persists that language skills are proven by using fake accents and an intensive use of idioms as this seemingly proves that the speaker has extensive experience in international communication and a profound insight into the language culture. He uses the language not only as a tool but adopts it as part of his professional socialization.

In Germany, foreign language skills and especially English have a high educational and professional significance in post-war generations. Historically, this significance originates from the strong cultural ties that were established soon after WWII with the English-speaking world and especially with the USA. Therefore, if a tourist from an English-speaking country who has very little knowledge of German, encounters a German, the German will instantly and un-

---

[10] Cf. also: http://en.wikipedia.org/wiki/Cautionary_tales (27.09.2011)

hesitatingly switch to English upon recognizing the tourist's linguistic background. Without being biased, I guess that the odds for the same experience in, for example, France are fewer. Moreover, the German society is prone to integrate Anglicisms and even full English idioms into their own language.[11]

Having said that, it is understandable that among pilots the language skills as part of a professional self-conception sometimes lead to linguistic over-compliance. Or to put it quite simply: sometimes pilots as well as other participants in aeronautic communication deviate from standard phraseology just to show off. Of course this can also cause problems since accents, idiomatic expressions, etc. often do not conform to the ICAO standard.

It is common among pilots to underline their route competence by referring to, for example, a navigation aid by its full name that often represents a local denomination of the place where the navigational aid is set up. Usually, and according to ICAO standard phraseology, those navigational aids are abbreviated by three-letter-codes like FFM for the Frankfurt VOR[12] navigational beacon or RUD for the Rüdesheim NDB[13] (both located in the vicinity of the FTSK Germersheim institute). In standard communication those navigational aids should be referred to by the phonetic alphabet so that the FFM VOR becomes Foxtrot-Foxtrot-Mike and the Rüdesheim beacon Romeo-Uniform-Delta. Thus a misunderstanding or difficulties in the acoustic perception of those names that are often names in a local (non ICAO, here German) language or peculiarities in the individual linguistic pronunciation are avoided. However, it is common that both, pilots and controllers, use the full name in their daily communication. For instance, British Controllers clear aircraft to fly to "Brookman Park" (BKP, a VOR in the London vicinity) or pilots flying over the Mediterranean Sea report their position as inbound to "Skopolos" (a beacon set up on the Greek Mediterranean Island of the same name). In this context it is remarkable that French air traffic control executes a very stern and thorough use of the three letter codes of all the navigational aids in France. It is understandable that for

---

[11] In this context I may briefly refer to the long on-going national debate about whether this is an identification of globalization or a self-abandonment of linguistic assertiveness as a "crown witness" to the above thesis of a general disposition in Germany towards the English language.

[12] VOR = Very High Frequency band Omnidirectional Range is a type of radio navigational system that allows to directly determine the aircraft position relative to the Earth's (usually magnetic) North; cf. also: http://en.wikipedia.org/wiki/VHF_omnidirectional_range (27.09.2011)

[13] NDB = Non Directional Beacon is another type of radio navigational system that provides directional information only relative to the beacon station; to combine this bearing with a direction to the Earth's North an additional compass instrument is needed; cf. also: http://en.wikipedia.org/wiki/Non-directional_beacon (27.09.2011)

non-French speakers the full name of "Angers" for the AGN VOR or "Sauveterre" for SAU VOR is not always easy to understand as its individual French pronunciation is special (especially the French proper name Angers has nothing in common with how it is pronounced and what it means in English). Here Alpha-Golf-November or Sierra-Alpha-Uniform is clear to everyone familiar with the basic ICAO phonetic alphabet. Ironically, it can often be heard over France that the French Controller dutifully clears a non-French aircraft to Alpha-Golf-November and the non-French pilot of this aircraft reads the clearance back with the full proper name.

More than just a profound display of route competence, this common deviation is meant as a gesture of the pilots flying in foreign airspace to address the local identity or to establish a sociable relationship with the local controller. Basically, the personnel in the aviation business shares a common techno-cultural esprit de corps as specialists. Here the deviation reflects a courteous or amicable inter-human approach, for which the technocratic and aseptic ICAO standard phraseology usually does not leave any room. Another impetus for this deviation is simply meant to break up the routine. Here my personal favorite is a navigational aid in Wyoming/USA (some 350 miles north of Denver) that is abbreviated CZI and should be referred to as Charlie-Zulu-India. However its full name is just more fun: "Crazy Woman"; it presumably refers to an ancient Native American name and is one of few navigational beacons that has been given an own reference on the Internet[14] (an honor that is not granted to many others of the 1.033 navigational installations in the USA, although they sometimes, too, have strange names like, for example, "Rattlesnake" / RSK in – not surprisingly – the New Mexico desert).

This over-compliance again is a normal variation of communicational behavior. To really believe that it would be possible to decouple the professional archetype of pilots or Air Traffic Controllers from the characteristics of their individual personality and especially from these irrational (but normal) elements of human behavior is naive. It would imply downgrading the facets of human behavior as disruptive and abnormal and that safety can only be achieved when human performance is phased to a machinelike routine. This is not an approach that is supported in CRM trainings. Again these deviations are generally accepted and respected as a normal by-product of human performance. The CRM approach on how to handle these deviations is to establish a careful consideration and monitoring of the communicational situation and its potential misunderstandings in order to fall back to ICAO standard communication whenever over-compliance is deemed critical. Again, re-applying this standard proves that the pilot (or controller) actively recovers control of the situation before a communicational mis-

---

[14] cf.: http://en.wikipedia.org/wiki/Crazy_Woman_Creek (27.09.2011)

conception becomes independent. This means that whenever one participant in the communication talks about "Crazy Woman" and the other is in doubt about whether both parties have a common understanding, the reconfirmation of this understanding is the adequate active contribution to eliminate potential confusion. A sole assumption about what the speaker means is not an acceptable and effective way of handling this situation. For the reconfirmation, and in order to avoid a further deepening, the ICAO standard phraseology forms the common and established basis. To ask back: "confirm Charlie-Zulu-India" does not expose the other part as inexperienced or insecure. Instead it underlines a high degree of professionalism and situational awareness.

Remarkably, and in contrast to the common deviation, pilot and controllers usually exercise an accurate use of standard phraseology whenever misunderstandings are foreseeable. This accredits that despite the common deviation the actors have a careful understanding about the necessity of standard communication in error-prone situations. For example, navigational beacons in Asia and China are rarely referred to by their proper name, especially not when the name represents a denomination in the local language. The potential for misunderstanding is just too obvious. A strict use of the three-letter-codes in the ICAO phonetic alphabet can be observed. The fall-back to austere standard communication can be seen whenever the technical quality of the transmission is impaired. This occurs, for example, in the oceanic airspace. Radio transmissions in the Very High Frequency band[15] offer clear quality, however the range is limited to approximately a line-of-sight between the transmitter and the receiver (due to the fact that the aircraft is flying in a high altitude, this line-of-sight is hereby extended so that the range, depending on the aircraft's actual altitude, can cover distances of up to 250 miles). When overflying oceanic areas the distance between the transmitter and the receiver usually exceeds the range of VHF equipment. Therefore decameter (High Frequency/HF) band radios are the equipment of choice. Their advantage over VHF is that the radio waves are refracted by the Earth's ionosphere and therefore can cover the long distances over the oceans (and even farther).[16] The disadvantage is that the radio waves are often disturbed by natural factors (for example daylight, solar activities), thus the transmission quality is limited or poor. This quality reduction is compensated by a rigid phraseology and syntax for every HF communication. The strict adherence to this standard makes the communication items (not the content of cause) foreseeable; each communication follows an assigned syntax and each item in the communication like aircraft call sign, geographic position, altitude and speed has an assigned place and exact wording in this syntax.

---

[15] cf.: http://en.wikipedia.org/wiki/Very_high_frequency (27.09.2011)
[16] For complete information: http://en.wikipedia.org/wiki/High_frequency (27.09.2011)

4 Improving Communication

After having given some insight into the possible background of deviations from the standard phraseology, according to what I experienced in my work, I would now like to present some thoughts on the role of communication and deviation from it, as well as provisions, in the context of CRM, to improve communication.

4.1 The Role of Human Performance

Let us start with some good news: up to now, there has not been an accident where both an emergency situation and deviation from standard phraseology have been identified as major causes. However, deviation can sometimes be traced as a contributing or side factor.

This is in line with modern research on safety. New approaches are developed to explain the reasons for a system to fail or to work well. I would especially like to refer to the work of Hollnagel et al. (2006), who base their research on human performance as an indifferent distinguishing mark. They do not share what can be called an *engineering point of view*, which pictures human beings simply as some sort of operators, whose performance can only deteriorate or ruin a situation and therefore must be excluded to the greatest possible extent from interferences with the technical system by a high level of automation. This conception was popular when aircraft manufacturers introduced complex computer automation in the cockpit. The European manufacturer Airbus, who became a forerunner in this conception, is known for the euphemistic statement that in his aircraft the pilots will be the most expensive passengers. Modern safety research opposes this conception of the human role in safety systems. Human performance is equally understood as an active contribution to safety that can also stop or invert an erratic course of the system or can prevent failure or its aggravation. Failure of a system is seen as an interaction of several causes and not as an event that can be explained by one reason only (cf. Hollnagel 2001: 3). Human performance in safety-sensitive systems is understood as firstly indifferent, failure is a normal by-product of this performance. Hence the deviation from standard phraseology must be considered normal, too. But it can become a threat when it is combined with other systemic failures. I have given numerous examples above that display that a deviation from standard communication follows utmost human characteristics and often enough is an understandable variation (under real life conditions) of an ideal picture. Other examples show that these indifferent characteristics and variations become erroneous in a combination with other factors.

4.2 Provisions for Communication Improvement in CRM

From a technical point of view, standard phraseology is a tool to maintain or reestablish a limited but commonly clear radio communication. It should be chosen whenever there is a need to eliminate or minimize potential communicational errors or misunderstanding from such a combination of risk factors. Its advantage is that this active contribution to safety is easily accessible. It does not require any in-depth thinking or complex decision-making. Since it is part of standard training for every pilot and air traffic controller it is within easy and direct reach and a consolidating measure against a sneaking corruption of communicational behavior and resilience.

Another important point is *risk awareness*, similar to situational awareness, mentioned above. With the help of CRM training, crew members can raise their awareness of risk situations, factors contributing to these situations and possibilities to resolve them. Risk awareness is the cornerstone in the development and training of an active *threat and error management*, which mainly comprises a constant review of and balancing between what I do and the risk this can imply. As a rule of thumb threat and error management can be imagined as two constant questions to oneself: 1. "What do I do?" 2. "Why do I do it?" Whenever a reasonable answer to only one of the questions cannot be found at first glance, the current decision-making or situational awareness should be carefully examined and observed. In terms of communication and deviation from standard communication this leads to the questions "Do I still communicate in standard phraseology?" 2. "Why do I deviate from standard phraseology?"

Apart from these cognitive skills, constant training in communication skills is still essential. This does not only mean that aviation personnel know the standard phraseology, but that they also accept that this standard is limited in its use. It is a standard for standard situations. In these predefined situations, however, its meaning is very clear. Therefore the question whether to deviate from it or not, has to be carefully considered on the one hand. On the other hand, deviation cannot be excluded from the outset. Non-standard situations might need or even call for non-standard communication.

As an example, the deviation *request priority* has to be mentioned once again. In a non-native speaker environment (e.g., Greece, Egypt, China), this deviation can have Babylonian misunderstanding, since the expression may be unknown and thus neither adequate reactions nor procedures are defined that could be applied. Here, adhering to standard phraseology upholds a commonly clear communication. The consequence is that whenever a situation is urgent or critical in terms of time, PAN-PAN or MAYDAY is the standard wording of choice. A colloquial phrase like "request priority" bears the threat that the other part in the communication will not recognize this transmission as a potential sub-message or encrypted message for urgency or even emergency situations – provided that it is understood at all.

5 Conclusion: Deviation – Acceptable or not?

Referring to Hollnagel et al. (2006) again, it can be said that, from a *threat and error management* perspective, standard phraseology is an indifferent factor. It can – and most of the time will – be of help and uphold a high and reliable level of safety. However, there are certain situations perceivable or even foreseeable, in which standard phraseology can have a limiting effect. In such cases, a deviation that offers additional informational content is not only an acceptable, but sometimes an even necessary option.

However, oversimplification, justification, deception or over-compliance usually do not indicate such an option by themselves. Deviation from standard phraseology can never be a rule but just the exception to it under very limited and special circumstances. But even under these options standard phraseology should form the consolidated frame around the necessary deviation.

To decide whether deviation is acceptable or not, recourse to risk awareness as well as threat and error management has to be made. And here Crew Resource Management again comes into play.

The author is pilot with TUIfly airlines, the German airline branch of the TUI travel group. After completion of his studies in law he joined the aviation industry in 1999 as a pilot. He soon became an instructor for Crew Resource Management (CRM) training, a mandatory training item for all aviation crews and technical aviation personnel. Since 2011 he is TUIfly's Chief Instructor for CRM and Human Factors training. He lives in Düsseldorf.

References

Beere, Ken (2005): *The Bluffer's Guide to the Flight Deck*. London: Oval Books.

CAA (2006): *Crew Resource Management (CRM) Training. Guidance for Flight Crew, CRM Instructors (CRMIS) and CRM Instructor-Examiners (CRMIES)*. Published by TSO (The Stationery Office) on behalf of the UK

Civil Aviation Authority. http://www.caa.co.uk/docs/33/CAP737.PDF [11.8.2011].

Hollnagel, Erik (2001): "Anticipating Failures: What Should Predictions Be About?", in: *The Human Factor in System Reliability – Is Human Performance Predictable?* RTO Meeting Proceedings 32, RTO-MP-32, January, Cedex, France, RTO, NATO. http://ftp.rta.nato.int/public// PubFulltext/RTO/MP/RTO-MP-032///MP-032-$KN.pdf [11.8.2011].

Hollnagel, Erik/David D. Woods/Nancy Leveson (ed.) (2006): *Resilience Engineering. Concepts and Precepts.* Ashgate Publishing Ltd.

Yerkes, Robert M./John D. Dodson (1908): "The Relation of Strength of Stimulus to Rapidity of Habit-Formation", in: *Journal of Comparative Neurology and Psychology*, 18 (5), 459-482.

Alice Müller-Leonhardt

"...Words Were Originally Magic..."
Constructiv(ist) Thinking about Language with Regard to Incident Investigation

1 Introduction

Based on the constructivist Steve de Shazer, who developed the Solution Focused Brief Therapy, this contribution addresses the solution-focused effect of words and language. The title of this article is borrowed from de Shazer's book on the constructivist use of language, which in turn is based on the conclusion of Sigmund Freud, who, in 1915, re-discovered the magic of words:

> "[...] Words were originally magic, and to this day words have retained much of their ancient magical power. By words one person can make another blissfully happy or drive him to despair. [...] Words provoke affects and are in general the means of mutual influence among men." (Freud 1915-1917, in: de Shazer 1994: 3)

De Shazer adds that words, and also silences, gestures, facial expressions, etc., are a part of language. Further, he assumes that "To look at the magic of words, we need to look at language, the context within which words work their magic" (de Shazer 1994: 3).

In High Reliability Organizations (HROs) such as Deutsche Flugsicherung (DFS) and other Airtraffic Navigation Services Providers (ANSPs) incident investigation is used to find sources of errors and to learn from them (Weick/Sutcliffe 2007). One of the instruments HROs use is a reporting system which not only reports errors that escalated to crisis proportions but also reports potential errors before they have a chance to escalate (such as EVAIR, cf. Stankovic this volume). Incident investigators use this instrument to try to understand the incidents or to reconstruct them so they can identify their sources. Language within this context represents interaction which occurred before, during and after an incident. However, normally the use of language in these investigations is focused on problems.

> "Resources for quality control and operational safety are directed primarily at finding out what went wrong in the past, rather than assuring that it will go right in the future. The focus is on diagnosis, not change." (Dekker 2002: 180)

The constructivist use of language is not focused on problems but on constructing solutions. De Shazer's work is of interest to incident investigations because he focuses his questions on the well-functioning of a system. It is a solution-focused, pragmatic and successful approach to problem solving in a therapeutic context.

The purpose of this contribution is to introduce the constructivist view of language use, to present a promising methodology for problem solving and to explore whether this approach might be appropriate for incident investigation. The aim is to develop ideas about how incident investigation might benefit from the constructivist use of language.

2 Constructivist Use of Language

2.1 Constructivist View

The common view on language describes the ability to perceive the truth of reality and to express this experience in words. De Shazer (1994) claims that in traditional Western thought, language is generally viewed as somehow being a representation of reality and that the science of language and the science of meaning are developed by looking behind and beneath the words to find the truth. He finds

> "...the common-sense assumption is that language is a transparent medium expressing already existing facts, i.e., when we use the term "tree", or "river", or "marital problem", or "sexual problem", or "depression", what the term means is known, is set ahead of time and for all time. The meaning of words is clear and unambiguous: a word refers directly to the thing itself." (de Shazer 1994: 7)

The constructivist view suggests that *language* is reality. The meaning of *marital problems*, *errors* and *failure* are the user's constructions of those terms. What these terms mean is both arbitrary and unstable, meaning varies depending on who is using the term and to whom it is being addressed within a specific context. Therefore de Shazer does not analyze language to acquire knowledge, but to find the benefits of using language to solve problems. In his view, writing and speaking are similar in regard to the use of language. The most obvious difference between reading and writing is that when reading the author is absent and when writing the reader is absent. Therefore in texts meanings cannot be delivered reliably. The objective knowledge one thinks is being transferred must always be interpreted by the reader. Every text has the potential to be misinterpreted. Dekker (2002) states that

> "Reading in post-structuralism is not seen as a passive consumption of what is already there, provided by somebody who possessed the truth and is only passing it on. Rather, reading is a creative act, a constitutive act, in which readers generate meanings out of their own experience and history with the text and with what it points to." (Dekker 2011: 21)

What is received is not necessarily what is sent. A simple sentence like the following quotation from a report of an air-traffic controller after two near misses illustrates the gap.

> "An anticipating planning was not possible for me for already a longer period of time." (Perret 2007: 161, translated from German by the author)

How can I, as the reader, interpret this sentence? Did the air-traffic controller have a personal problem? What does he mean by *anticipating planning*? In what context and time frame was it impossible to make a plan? What was the message?

Following the description of Perret the air-traffic controller did not get the necessary support in a very dynamic air-traffic situation because there was no other colleague available. Perret does not make clear what the above quoted sentence means (Perret 2007: 161).

The second example is described in the following sentence:

> "It is the duty of an organization not to leave a staff member, who made a mistake, namely a mistake with huge consequences, alone and to care for him." (Perret 2007: 210, translated from German by the author)

This quotation from a manager of a European ANSP demonstrates the effects of one's choice of words and even possible double-bind messages. At first it appears to indicate that he really cares for staff members. A second message includes that staff members are free to commit individual mistakes with huge consequences within a complex system.

In that case a single person had to pay for the huge consequences although there is no evidence for individual failure. Therefore, also, language and words in context of accident and/or incident investigation reports is a very important factor.

2.2 Dealing with Power and Misunderstanding

Following the assumption of Foucault (1980) that power is *omnipresent*, de Shazer (1994: 59) finds that individuals are always and everywhere in the same position, simultaneously undergoing, exercising, and resisting power in a net of systemic relationships among a network of systems. Following Emerson (1964) he assumes

"...if the amount of power necessary is dependent on the amount of resistance necessary to overcome it, then when there is cooperation rather than resistance, the need for power is obviously diminished accordingly." (de Shazer 1994: 61)

Therefore, cooperation is seen as an important factor in a successful problem solving process, while resistance is an indicator of power. De Shazer also assumes that in every situation, misunderstanding is more probable than understanding. However, in his view it is misunderstanding which makes a conversation possible because misunderstanding may be used to construct mutually satisfactory solutions.

2.3 Words and Language as Constructivist Instruments

In de Shazer's constructivist approach, the way questions are asked is a central issue within the problem solving process. These questions ask for exceptions, differences or the opportunity to act differently in the context of a problem. De Shazer's claim to fame was especially aided by the development of the *miracle question*.

"Suppose that tonight after you go to sleep a miracle happens and the problems [...] are solved immediately. [...] Once you wake up tomorrow morning, how will you discover that a miracle has happened? Without your telling them, how will other people know that a miracle has happened?" (de Shazer 1994: 95)

In his view this miracle question is a way to begin constructing a bridge between the one who asks and the one who answers.

"The phrasing of the question includes a radical distinction between problem and solution, which is a result of our noticing that the development of a solution is not necessarily related to the problems and complaints in any way [...]. The absence (of the complaint/problem) is a given and the client is being asked to describe an effect [...]." (de Shazer 1994: 95)

3 Conclusions and Suggestions

In this constructivist view, air-traffic controllers who are participating in incident investigation know the situation and the interaction concerning an incident best. They therefore should be seen as experts in the situation.

ANSPs would benefit if incident investigators developed questions using constructivist language. The answers could lead to the mutual development of problem solving strategies for critical situations.

Following the constructivist view, questions focusing on differences, scaling questions or questions about the context could lead to solutions.

For example,

"Why did it make sense to you to act the way you did in this situation?"

"How could their actions have made sense?" (Dekker 2002: 54)

The incident investigation process should be cooperative, and misunderstanding should be regarded as a condition of the mutual problem solving process. These resulting reports could contain answers which go beyond the individual description of an incident.

As investigators are colleagues, they are in a different situation than external counselors. Having to deal with a complex socio-technical system, it is convenient to be familiar with the system and the proceedings. However, although investigators are experts in the operational situation, they need to maintain their distance and avoid focusing on their own views.

Weick and Sutcliffe (2007) believe that through their ongoing interactions, staff members produce hypotheses about what is actually happening, what action can be taken, and what the long-term systemic outcomes of these acts could be. They conclude that the production of hypotheses contains the potential to cope with surprises, which are part of a complex system. Then, using reflection on existing hypotheses should be part of the sense-making process within incident investigation.

Weick and Sutcliffe (2007) also found that incident investigators should have different expectations of and perspectives on the investigated situation. As a sociologist and investigator of accidents, Vaughan (2005) also proposes to integrate social–psychological scientists into investigations to add an external view. Further studies should integrate this interdisciplinary aspect heading to create divers teams trained in constructivist use of language for incident investigations.

Based on the presupposition that incidents within HROs provide information about the well-functioning of the system, constructivist use of language has the potential to contribute to the optimization of incident investigations adding an interactive solution-focused approach. This requires us to follow Steve de Shazer saying: "Freud was wrong, words have lost none of their magic" (de Shazer 1994: 50).

Alice Müller-Leonhardt holds a diploma in Educational Sciences. She is a systemic consultant (Institut für Familientherapie Weinheim), a Critical Incident Stress Management (CISM) trainer (International Critical Incident Stress Foundation), faculty member of the Resiliency Sciences Institute (RSI) of the University of Maryland, Baltimore County (UMBC) and a member of the Resilience Engineering Association (REA). Alice Müller-Leonhardt currently works at the work and engineering psychology group at Technische Universität Darmstadt. She works on her doctoral thesis with focus on soft factors creating resilience in complex systems; one of these is language in incident investigation.

References

De Shazer, Steve (1994): *Word Were Originally Magic*. New York: Norton & Company.

Dekker, Sidney (2002): *The Field Guide to Human Error Investigations*. Aldershot, UK: Ashgate.

Dekker, Sidney (2011): *Drift into failure. From Hunting Broken Components to Understanding Complex Systems*. Aldershot, UK: Ashgate.

Emerson, Richard (1964): "Power-Dependence Relations: Two Experiments", *Sociometry* 27.3, 282-298.

Foucault, Michel (1980): *Power/Knowledge. Selected Interviews and Other Writings, 1972-1977*. New York: Pantheon.

Perret, Ariane (2007): *Kollision aus heiterem Himmel. Die Flugzeugkatastrophe von Überlingen*. Zürich: Orell Füssli.

Vaughan, Diane W. (2005): "System Effects: On Slippery Slopes, Repeating Negative Patterns, and Learning from Mistakes", in: Starbuck, William/Moshe Farjoun, (ed.): *Organization at the Limit: NASA and the Columbia Accident*. Oxford: Blackwell.

Weick, Karl E./Kathleen M. Sutcliffe (2007). *Managing the Unexpected: Resilient Performance in an Age of Uncertainty*, 2nd edition. San Francisco: Jossey-Bass.

Silvia Hansen-Schirra

Linguistic Dominance in Air Traffic Control

1 The Nature of Aviation Communication

From a linguistic point of view, aviation communication is an interesting object of research since it integrates different research questions in a very specialized and isolated language variety:

First of all, it is categorized as language for specific purposes (LSP). More precisely, it is a controlled language since it exhibits both restricted vocabulary and phraseology. Controlled languages are sub-languages within certain domains created in order to avoid ambiguities and ensure fast and efficient comprehensibility. Thus, they serve to produce consistent and clearly understandable texts for the purpose of technical documentation or for (semi-) automatic translation (Huijsen 1998). For aviation communication, the standard phraseology is defined by the ICAO (International Civil Aviation Organization[1]; cf. also Koble/Roh and Fox this volume). Controlled languages are also widespread in the technical documentation of the aviation industry (e.g. the ASD Simplified Technical English; ASD-STE100 2010) including company-specific adaptations (e.g. Wojcik et al. 1998 for Boeing) and tools for checking controlled languages (e.g. the Boeing Simplified English Checker[2]).

Secondly, although there are a number of official ICAO languages[3], English is used as a lingua franca in aviation communication. This may result, on the one hand, in changes in language use caused by interferences from other languages. On the other hand, several comprehensibility difficulties occur, the main problem being a large amount of non-native speakers. Problems of English as a lingua franca (ELF) are discussed in other domains as well (e.g. Mollin 2006 for Euro-English or Ventola/Mauranen 1996 for academic writing). In order to improve the language skills of pilots and controllers, proficiency levels and examinations were introduced by ICAO (cf. Rees and Hinz/Sturges this volume for a more detailed discussion). Still, since most of the time the dialogues between controllers and pilots are fast and out of context and undergo a hectic, loud and disturbed atmosphere, the comprehensibility of utterances is problematic and cannot always be taken for granted. Another problem is caused by the fact that

---
[1] http://www2.icao.int/en/home/default.aspx
[2] http://www.boeing.com/phantom/sechecker/index.html
[3] Besides English, the following languages are officially allowed: Arabic, Chinese, French, Russian and Spanish (cf. Fox this volume).

pilots and controllers may use – whether officially accepted or not – other languages as well, without knowing whether other pilots nearby know the involved language. This disturbs the transparency of the communication and might lead to communication problems for approaching pilots. Another effect could be that pilots and controllers switch from one language to the other. This phenomenon is called code-mixing (cf. Auer 1998) and might also lead to comprehensibility problems.

The third interesting research question arises from the fact that a written standard is mainly to be applied to the spoken channel. Phraseology and vocabulary which function well in written context might cause problems when spoken aloud, especially within hectic and out-of-context situations. Non-applicability of the written code in terms of speech rates results in short cuts (Peters 2010) or repetitions (cf. Bieswanger this volume). This also means that phonetic articulation and language comprehension have to be trained (which is mostly not the case for other controlled languages). In addition, the discrepancies between written standard and spoken conversation also become visible when it comes to the pragmatics of language (cf. Leech 1983 and Sahliger/Renn this volume): strict and impersonal phraseology works for written documents. When it comes to oral conversations, interactants tend to use phrases of politeness and greetings (see section 2). The lack of politeness might cause problems in intercultural communication which, in turn, might lead to non-communication.

Finally, the different speaker roles which are involved in aviation communication can be looked at from a linguistic point of view: the pilot takes the role of a recipient of orders; the controller is more in the position of issuing instructions. This social role relationship influences the dominance relations, which are again reflected in the language use of controllers and pilots (cf. Neumann 2008 for a detailed discussion of register variation concerning the level of authority and the level of expertise). Here, several linguistic features are involved: e.g. the choice of vocabulary or grammatical mood (i.e. the use of imperatives, declaratives, interrogatives) but also turn frequencies, etc. If the linguistic usage chosen by the interactants is inadequate or if it is regarded as inadequate because of cultural differences (cf. Bieswanger this volume) the imbalance between pilot and controller might cause misunderstanding as well as non-communication.

In the following, some of the characteristics described here are investigated on the basis of a corpus of transcribed aviation communication. This analysis does not focus on ICAO phraseology or the deviation from the standard but on the nature of aviation communication as a highly specialized form of expert communication. This means that linguistic dominance relations in Air Traffic Control (ATC) are of special interest for the analysis. The corpus under investigation contains recordings from the following airports: Paris-Orly Airport, Amsterdam

Airport Schiphol, John F. Kennedy International Airport and Brasilia International Airport. Each of the four different sub-corpora covers 10,000 tokens respectively. The recordings are taken from LiveATC[4], the transcriptions are based on GAT (cf. Selting et al. 1998; cf. also Fox this volume for a more detailed description of the corpus compilation process). The corpus is annotated for parts of speech (word classes) using the TreeTagger.[5] On the basis of this corpus, we first investigate the status of the English language as a lingua franca in aviation communication. In a second step, relevant linguistic features are extracted which shed light on linguistic dominance relations in ATC.

2 Lingua Franca Status

As mentioned above, the English language is used as a lingua franca in many different domains and areas all over the world (cf. Crystal 2003 or Mair 2003 for comprehensive discussions). This also holds true for aviation communication where English can be seen as the common language – especially in contexts of non-native communication. However, other languages are also officially accepted by ICAO (see above). Therefore, the question arises of how dominant the English language actually is. In the following, the differing habits in language use at John F. Kennedy International Airport, Paris-Orly Airport, Amsterdam Airport Schiphol and Brasilia International Airport are quantified. We have chosen these airports because of the differing language attitudes in the different countries: concerning Paris-Orly Airport, we expect a frequent usage of French because of its official ICAO status and the French language protection laws.[6] We assume Amsterdam Airport Schiphol with its 45.3 million passengers[7] as being more dependent on English as a lingua franca than Brasilia International Airport with its 14 million passengers.[8] Before we start discussing the results it should be mentioned that at JFK International Airport English was used in 100 % of cases. Since English is the official language of the USA this result is not surprising.

Figure 1 shows that the corpus analysis corroborates these hypotheses. At Paris-Orly Airport, French beats English by more than 10 %. French pilots and controllers tend to use French among native speakers; of course they switch to English when an international aircraft approaches. Interestingly enough we observe code-switching in 10 % of all utterances. In these cases typically phrases of politeness (e.g. "bonjour") or opening or closing formulas (e.g. "écoute" or

---

[4] http://www.LiveATC.net
[5] http://www.ims.uni-stuttgart.de/projekte/corplex/TreeTagger/
[6] http://www.legifrance.gouv.fr/affichTexte.do?cidTexte=LEGITEXT000005616341&dateTexte=20110906#
[7] http://en.wikipedia.org/wiki/Amsterdam_Airport_Schiphol
[8] http://en.wikipedia.org/wiki/Bras%C3%ADlia_International_Airport

"d'accord") are issued in French. Typically, in utterances where code-switching occurs digits are spelled out in English – the speaker probably wants to make sure that this information is clearly understood.

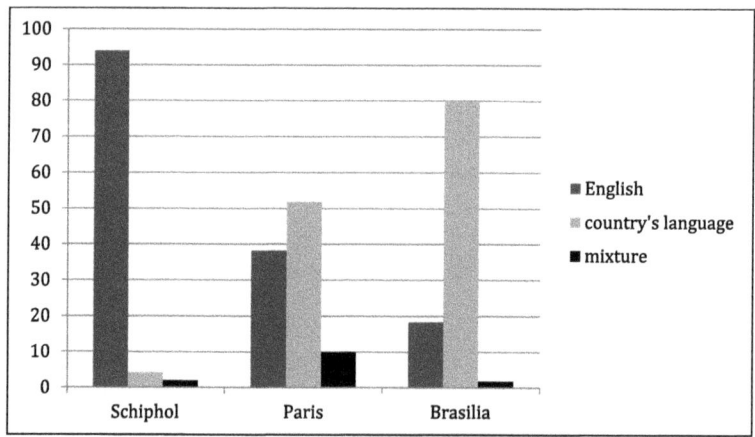

Figure 1: Language Distribution[9]

At Brasilia International Airport, Portuguese is the dominant language with 80 % of all utterances. English is used less frequently – especially for the pronunciation of digits. Again, the pilots tend to use English to make sure that the digits are understood properly. Code-switching only rarely occurs – national flights seem to be navigated in Portuguese only.

In contrast to this, at Amsterdam Airport Schiphol English is clearly the dominating language with more than 90 % of all utterances being made in English. Dutch is used for greeting formulas only, the same holds true for code-switching combining greetings with English messages, e.g. "goedemiddag, KLM four four Sierra, one eight center".

To conclude, English is of course an important language for aviation communication but it is not as dominant as one would assume. The frequency of its usage depends heavily on political language policy as well as the size and international character of the respective airport.

---

[9] Fox (this volume) reports similar findings for a smaller part of the corpus.

3 Linguistic Dominance in a Corpus of Aviation Communication

3.1 Turn Taking

In conversational analysis, the focus is on the organization and sequencing of turns and their allocation to different speakers. Since the qualitative analysis of turns (i.e. the classification in constructional vs. allocational components; cf. Sacks et al. 1974) requires deep and manual annotation we focus our quantitative study on the calculation of words per speaker, turns per speaker and words per turn. We assume that a higher frequency and density of words and turns can be allocated to the controllers, whose function is to provide the pilots with information and instructions.

		turns (%)	words (%)	words/turn
Schiphol	controllers	45.03	45.54	11.62
	pilots	54.97	54.46	11.38
JFK	controllers	41.95	60.00	20.6
	pilots	58.05	40.00	9.92

Table 1: Turn taking

Table 1 shows that our assumption cannot be verified: at Schiphol Airport a higher number of turns as well as words can be attributed to the pilots. Consequently, the number of words per turn is comparable for controllers and pilots.

A different picture emerges for JFK: here, controllers issue fewer turns but more words than pilots do. This leads to an extremely high number of words per turn for the controllers (20.6), whereas the pilots' figure is comparable to that of the pilots approaching Schiphol. This leads to the conclusion that JFK controllers need many more words to issue their instructions, which is obviously not indicative of dominance but rather of weakness or of a chaotic situation at JFK. To answer this question, deeper linguistic analyses (e.g. in terms of speech acts; cf. Austin 1962; Searle 1969) or other investigation methods (e.g. participant observation) are needed.

3.2 Grammatical Mood

Describing the relationship of level of authority and grammatical mood, Neumann (2008: 120) states the following:

> "A sender with a high level of authority should be in a position to make demands at his/her discretion. This may be reflected in an above average frequency of imperatives, used to express demands for goods and services. The opposite case, where the sender has a lower level of authority than the addressee, may also be found in the corpus. In this case, the

sender may simply provide information and use the declarative mood for this purpose; or s/he may demand information from the addressee and use interrogative mood. [...] we expect the declarative mood to be the neutral option [...]."

Based on the assumption that the pilot is more in the position of an information seeker and the controller has the function to issue instructions we expect a higher frequency of interrogatives for the pilots and a higher frequency of imperatives for the controllers (see *Table 2*).

		imperative (%)	interrogative (%)	declarative (%)
Schiphol	controllers	67	5	28
	pilots	2	6	92
JFK	controllers	39	4	57
	pilots	2	8	90

Table 2: Grammatical mood

Concerning the distribution of imperatives our hypothesis can be confirmed for both airports since their frequencies are higher in both sub-corpora of controllers' utterances. The following examples show imperatives frequently used by controllers: "hold...!", "turn...!", "climb...!", "descend...!", "remain...!", etc. The few imperatives issued by pilots include affirmation and confirmation requests: "affirm...!" and "confirm...!". It is, however, interesting that the Schiphol controllers are far more dominant than the ones at JFK, who use more neutral declaratives. One might assume that – because of reasons of politeness – they tend to use more plain language and fewer standardized ICAO phraseology (which triggers the use of imperatives); but to figure out the explanatory backgrounds for this difference we need other methods of investigation (e.g. questionnaires).

At JFK the pilots ask more questions than controllers at the same airport and compared to their colleagues approaching Schiphol. Again, this might reflect the probably more chaotic situation at JFK where more questioning is necessary (e.g. "Can you repeat?" or "Can we continue...?"). But to corroborate this assumption, again, more psycholinguistically oriented investigation methods need to be applied.

3.3 Lexical Choice

The lexical choice reveals the level of expertise of an interactant (cf. Neumann 2008). We use the calculation of lexical density and type-token ratio (cf. Hansen-Schirra 2008) to operationalize and compare the lexical choice of controllers and pilots. Lexical density (LD) means the ratio of lexical vs. grammatical words. It is calculated by first subtracting the number of function words, which can be identified through the part-of-speech tagging, from the total number of words. The number of lexical words thus obtained is divided by the total number of words and then multiplied by 100. The easier a text is, the lower the lexical density tends to be. This means that a high lexical density – i.e. more lexical words and fewer function words – indicates a high degree of lexical words (in the case of LSP mostly terms) and thus a high level of expertise. The corpus analysis will reveal whether this tendency also holds true for controlled languages.

The type-token ratio (TTR) is the ratio of different tokens vs. running words. This percentage is determined by dividing the number of lemmata (types) by the total number of words (tokens) and then multiplying the result by 100. This measure is an indicator of lexical variation: a low TTR indicates a low level of expertise since the texts exhibit only few different words. A high TTR in expert communication represents more lexical variation in general and more variation with respect to terminology in particular and thus a higher level of expertise. Since aviation communication is regarded as expert-to-expert discourse including a high level of expertise with extremely specialized dialogues we expect high values for both calculations.

As can be seen in *Table 3* our expectations concerning TTR are not fulfilled: both controllers and pilots exhibit a low TTR in comparison with register-neutral reference corpora (cf. 15.64 for the English reference corpus of the CroCo Corpus; Hansen-Schirra et al. forthcoming). At first glance, this seems to indicate a low level of expertise, but at second glance, this is a logical consequence of the use of the restricted ICAO vocabulary and phraseology. The low TTR values are caused by the standardized and pre-defined controlled language and testify to a high usage frequency of digits, repetitive vocabulary, call signs, etc.

		TTR	LD
Schiphol	controllers	11.37	84.52
	pilots	11.98	80.81
JFK	controllers	9.01	83.28
	pilots	9.42	77.86

Table 3: Lexical choice

In terms of LD, our hypothesis can be confirmed: we find above average values for both, controllers and pilots (cf. 57.49 for the English reference corpus of the CroCo Corpus; Hansen-Schirra et al. forthcoming). This is not surprising when we take into account that the usage of some function words (e.g. prepositions) is not allowed. Consequently, this means that both pilots and controllers use a high amount of lexical words including a high degree of terminology. For both airports under investigation, the figures for controllers are higher than those for pilots. This leads to the conclusion that controllers are slightly more dominant than pilots, who tend to use slightly more function words (e.g. interrogative pronouns).

4 Perspectives for Future Research

The aim of this article was to investigate linguistic dominance on the basis of a corpus of transcriptions which allows a comparison between pilots and controllers. The corpus analysis has shown that there is a dominance relationship in terms of language use, turn-taking, grammatical mood and lexical choice. The descriptive results have raised awareness to the fact that a balanced social role relationship between controllers and pilots plays an important role for successful aviation communication. Still, some results cannot be explained and some questions remain open.

Therefore, future research should combine corpus-based investigations with psycholinguistic methods, such as questionnaires, participant observations, video recordings of pilots and controllers as well as screen recordings. Furthermore, it would be interesting to employ eye-tracking to track the controllers' and pilots' eye movement. *Figure 2* shows an eye-tracking pilot study of a sample radar picture of Frankfurt Airport[10]. The dots are the fixations, while the lines represent the saccades of the gaze[11].

The eye-tracking results might indicate situations of cognitive overload, e.g. when the eye movements become hectic. Data triangulation (complementing eye-tracking results with questionnaires, etc.) might help to corroborate the experimental results. Such an integrated multi-method approach could provide explanations to the open questions addressed in the study above. On this basis, the cognitive modeling of aviation communication becomes possible including the identification of all participant roles and hierarchies and their influence on the efficiency and quality of ATC.

---

[10] Source of radar picture: http://www.dfs.de/dfs/internet_2008/module/presse/deutsch/ presse /mediathek/bilder/flugsicherungssysteme/radarbild_anflug_frankfurt.zip

[11] The pilot study was carried out at the Eye-Lab of the Translation Department, Mainz University, Germersheim.

Figure 2: Eye-tracking in ATC (simulation)

Silvia Hansen-Schirra serves as full professor and Chair of English Linguistics and Translation Studies at the translation department of the Mainz University in Germersheim (Germany). She was principal investigator of a research project in which aviation communication was investigated on the basis of linguistically annotated corpora.

References

ASD-STE100 (2010): "ASD Simplified Technical English. International Specification for the preparation of maintenance documentation in a controlled language", in: http://www.asd-ste100.org/ [Issue 5, April 2010].

Auer, Peter (1998): *Code-Switching in Conversation*. London: Routledge.

Austin, John L. (1962): *How to do Things with Words*. Cambridge: Harvard University Press.

Crystal, David (2003): *English as a Global Language*. Cambridge: Cambridge University Press.

Hansen-Schirra, Silvia (2008): *The Processing of Translated Text*. Habilitationsschrift, Saarland University.

Hansen-Schirra, Silvia/Stella Neumann/Erich Steiner (forthcoming): *Cross-linguistic Corpora for the Study of Translations. Insights from the Language Pair English-German*. Berlin/New York: de Gruyter.

Huijsen, Willem-Olaf (1998): "Controlled Language – An Introduction", in: *Proceedings of the Second International Workshop on Controlled Language Applications* (CLAW98), May 21-22. Pittsburgh, Pennsylvania: Language Technologies Institute, Carnegie Mellon University, 1-15.

Leech, Geoffrey N. (1983): *Principles of Pragmatics*. London: Longman.

Mair, Christian (ed.) (2003): *The Politics of English as a World Language*. Amsterdam: Rodopi.

Mollin, Sandra (2006): *Euro-English. Assessing Variety Status*. Tübingen: Narr.

Neumann, Stella (2008): *Contrastive Register Variation. A quantitative Approach to the Comparison of English and German*. Habilitationsschrift, Saarland University.

Peters, Christoph (2010): "Vor- und Nachteile von Abweichungen aus der Sicht des Fluglotsen". Talk presented at the Conference *Languages and cultures above the clouds – international English between standardization and everyday aviation communication*, 4th-5th November 2010, Germersheim.

Sacks, Harvey/Emanuel A. Schegloff/Gail Jefferson (1974): "A Simplest Systematics for the Organization of Turn Taking for Conversation", *Language* 50, 696-735.

Searle, John (1969): *Speech Acts*. Cambridge: Cambridge University Press.

Selting, Margret et al. (1998): "Gesprächsanalytisches Transkriptionssystem (GAT)", *Linguistische Berichte* 173, 91-122.

Ventola, Eija/Anna Mauranen (ed.) (1996): *Academic Writing. Intercultural and Textual Issues*. Amsterdam: Benjamins.

Wojcik, Richard/Heather Holmback/Jim Hoard (1998): "Boeing Technical English: An Extension of AECMA SE Beyond the Aircraft Maintenance Domain", in: *Proceedings of the Second International Workshop on Controlled Language Applications* (CLAW98), May 21-22. Pittsburgh, Pennsylvania: Language Technologies Institute, Carnegie Mellon University, 114-123.

Lynette Rees

The Role of Plain Language in English Training for French Air Traffic Controllers

1 Introduction

English language courses form an integral part of the training of air-traffic control officers in France whether as part of the initial training courses offered at the French Civil Aviation Academy in Toulouse (ENAC) or as on-the-job linguistic programs for qualified controllers. In both cases the courses are designed to enable the trainee or qualified controller to demonstrate a minimum ICAO level 4 for operational purposes or to achieve the extended level 5 on the ICAO scale. This field study draws upon my experience as an English language coordinator for the French civil aviation authority (DGAC) and will thus focus essentially on English language training programs for qualified controllers.

At each air navigation service or air control center in France, an English language coordinator is responsible for setting up the English language training programs for qualified controllers, harmonizing these programs on a local and national level as well as coordinating the English training courses for trainee controllers with ENAC. Each coordinator manages a team of teachers locally and the training might include group classes, tutorials and immersion courses abroad.

In accordance with the ICAO guidelines for aviation English training programs, the emphasis is put on the communicative approach to language learning with the objective being to improve speaking, listening and interactive skills. The main focus of the aviation English training is the domain of plain language in operational context which is defined in the ICAO guidelines as being situated "between the very narrow focus of standardized phraseology and the very wide focus of conversational aviation topics" (ICAO 2009: 1)

Plain language is an important component of radio-telephony communications. Although ICAO clearly states that ICAO phraseologies should always be used in the first instance (ICAO 2004: 2.4), it recognizes the need for plain language proficiency especially for non-routine situations. The second part of this article aims to demonstrate how everyday operations might give rise to the use of plain language by controllers and pilots alike.

2 The Impact of the Language Proficiency Requirements on English Training for ATC in France

2.1 The Development of English Training Courses

English training courses for qualified air-traffic controllers have existed in the different centers in France for some 30 years. Although English teachers were primarily recruited in the centers to ensure the continuity of the English training programs for trainee controllers following the ENAC sandwich course, qualified controllers could also attend courses on a voluntary basis.

Following the 1998 ICAO Assembly resolution A32-16 concerning English language proficiency in air traffic communications, and in accordance with the Eurocontrol (2002) Safety Regulatory Requirement ESARR 5, level assessments, created by working groups composed of linguistic and operational experts, were carried out at regular intervals with a view to defining training requirements. The introduction of the ICAO language proficiency requirements in 2003 made it henceforth imperative to ensure all controllers would be capable of demonstrating an operational level 4 in time for the ICAO 2008 deadline.

As a result, the training courses have gradually become more structured with the introduction of individual language programs.

2.2 The Implementation of Individual Language Programs

The initial aim of individual training programs was to bring all controllers up to an ICAO level 4. However, since 2008 the objective has changed slightly and is now one of maintaining this level or of attaining a level 5.

An individual interview enables a training program to be defined for each controller. This program is presented to the controller in the form of a document. The first page of the document corresponds to an appreciation of the controller's linguistic skills and sets out the specific points, grammatical or other that have to be worked on. The second page details the number of hours and types of courses to be followed over a specific time period.

Depending on the controller's level, a level 4 or a level 5, the controller will respectively have a minimum of 75 hours to do over a course of three years or 100 hours to do over a course of six years, following the ICAO recommendation (ICAO 2004: A.1) that pilots and controllers demonstrating a level 4 should be evaluated at least once every three years and those with a level 5, once every six years.

Controllers with a level 6 are also provided with a training program over 6 years, even though they are exempt from re-sitting the licensing test.

2.3 In-house Training Programs: Organization, Resources and Content

The types of courses offered at each center might take various forms depending on the human and technical resources available. The controllers attend group classes as well as one-to-one sessions and follow a mix of intensive and extensive courses. This is particularly beneficial as the objective differs in each case. An intensive course might help the student progress more rapidly, but it's the extensive training that will enable the student to best maintain the level over a longer period of time, as language learning is an ongoing process. The courses might take place in a normal classroom situation, in a language lab or using the ATC simulators.

The *Manual on the Implementation of ICAO Language Proficiency Requirements* (ICAO 2004: 7.2.2) recognizes three distinct roles of language as a factor in aviation accidents and incidents:

- the use of phraseologies
- the proficiency in plain language
- the use of more than one language

Within the French civil aviation authority (DGAC) phraseology, which is considered a distinct discipline in the operational domain, is taught by ATC instructors. The role of the aviation English trainer is thus primarily to improve proficiency in plain language using a communicative approach to language learning in order to facilitate communication. The aviation English trainer might also help the controller improve their linguistic and cross-cultural awareness, self-confidence in English and situational sensitivity.

The courseware used is developed by the trainers themselves with the aid of subject matter experts using live traffic recordings and other subject matter that closely reflects the situations controllers have to deal with in their professional lives. This has the advantage of rendering the training more effective and motivating. The topics covered range from aircraft parts and technical problems to medical problems and air rage.

The ultimate aim is to help controllers deal effectively with all the non-standard, abnormal or emergency situations for which standardized phraseology proves insufficient.

3 The Importance of the Plain Language Component in Improving Fluency and Reducing Misunderstandings

The ICAO language proficiency requirements, consisting of a set of holistic descriptors and the operational level 4 on the rating scale, were adopted by the ICAO Council in March 2003. Applicable to the use of both phraseologies and plain language, these requirements were designed to be used as a frame of reference for teachers and to provide a greater consistency within the language standards of pilots and air-traffic controllers worldwide.

Although ICAO clearly states that ICAO phraseologies should always be used in the first instance, it recognizes "a need for plain language proficiency as a fundamental component of radiotelephony communications" (ICAO 2004: 2.4).

Whereas the role of plain language may seem quite obvious in the case of emergency situations, it may seem less critical in everyday routine situations. However, a controller's everyday tasks of sharing information and negotiating various matters might frequently lead him or her to resort to plain language.

Therefore, when plain language competency is improved, misunderstandings can be reduced on a daily basis. This point might be illustrated by looking in turn at the four fundamental skills on the ICAO scale.

3.1 Pronunciation

To demonstrate an operational level 4, ICAO does not require pilots and controllers to have "native-like" pronunciation but rather to work towards having a pronunciation that is "intelligible to the wider international aeronautical community" (ICAO 2004: 2.7.5). Work on pronunciation should be consistent throughout the English training and controllers should be encouraged to speak slowly and clearly as rate of speech as well as accent can hinder communication. Research has shown that when two non-native English speakers are communicating they will actually rely more on pronunciation than on context. In voice-only communication the role of pronunciation is further accentuated.

Our training programs include activities to enhance sound awareness, for example, identifying the common sound in a group of words, work on minimal pairs (a pair of words that differ only in one sound) and categorizing words according to individual sounds, as well as work on syllable stress and intonation. Controllers need to be aware of some homographs i.e. words that have the same spelling but a slightly different stress. Here are some examples that can be found on the Skybrary website (http://www.skybrary.aero):

conte'nt (*accept*), co'ntent (*things: inside*); refu'se (*disagree*), re'fuse (*rubbish*); clo**s**e (-z) (*shut*), close (*near*)

A word when mispronounced might not be recognizable thus making the whole sentence incomprehensible:

*Could you send a **haircut** (?) to our aircraft?* – The pilot was in fact requesting an **air cart**

When contractions and '*ed*' inflections are mispronounced the time frame for the action might be misunderstood:

*We '**ve** tax**ied** to the holding point* (the aircraft is at the holding point)
vs.
We_ taxi_ to the holding point (understood as the aircraft is taxiing at the moment of speaking)

3.2 Structure

The teaching of grammatical structures can be based around the communicative functions which have been recognized as being dominant in radiotelephony communications.

The 4 categories are:

- Communicative functions directed towards triggering actions such as orders, requests and offers to act, advice, permission/approval;
- Communicative functions directed towards sharing information, the information to be shared could concern present facts, the future or past events, necessity and feasibility;
- Communicative functions directed towards managing the pilot-controller relationship, these could include such functions as complaining, apologizing and expressing satisfaction;
- Communicative functions directed towards managing the dialogue.

ICAO stresses that importance should be placed on global errors, those which interfere with meaning rather than local errors which do not, and emphasizes the use of direct rather than indirect structures and the importance of being explicit.

Indeed, interrupting and correcting each grammar error is likely to have a negative effect on fluency resulting in the person actually becoming more hesitant.

In the same way as the other skills, grammatical structures are best practiced using communicative activities such as role-playing rather than traditional written exercises. For example, narrative tenses and reported speech might be practiced through story telling or summarizing while prediction activities can be used to improve the use of the simple future and modals. Speculating around pictures and texts about incidents might enhance the use of conditionals and past modals.

On an almost daily basis controllers must master the language functions necessary to negotiate situations as diplomatically as possible. What phraseology could a controller use, for example, to reply to the pilot below?

I know it's not your fault, but it's been twenty minutes since I asked for push and the tow bar was stolen from me to go and push a flight which is nowhere near ready to go and is not even listening out on frequency.

3.3 Vocabulary

The vocabulary related to aviation communication is vast. A list of lexical domains can be found in appendix B of the ICAO *Manual on the implementation of ICAO Language Proficiency Requirements*.

The ICAO recommends avoiding the use of informal jargon and idioms whenever possible. However, some work on idiomatic phrasal verbs to increase the controller's awareness of those most used in an aeronautical context could help the controller understand certain pilot messages and avoid misunderstandings.

*The passenger has just **passed out**. (= to faint)*
vs.
*The passenger has just **passed away**. (= to die)*

*We **took** a bird **out** just over the runway. (= to have a bird strike)*

*We are **running out of** (= to be low on) fuel and we are going to have to **put** the plane **down** (= to land) wherever it happens to be.*

*Our left-hand brake unit is indicating very hot and could **spark off** (= to ignite) a fire.*

*Our flight has been **put off** for an hour. (= to postpone)*

Controllers must also be aware of homonyms, words that have the same sound and spelling but a different meaning.

Taxi = helicopter (hover taxi, air taxi) / to move
Aircraft = one or many aircraft (no plural form)
Gate = location at the terminal building / point in the sky
Roll = pivot in the air about longitudinal axis / forward movement
Go ahead = urge speaking / forward motion

Stand by = wait for information / standing
(examples taken from the Skybrary website)

Activities for vocabulary acquisition can be very varied ranging from labeling diagrams or pictures (e.g. plane parts, an airport terminal, the human body), matching words with definitions or guessing the word corresponding to a definition to all sorts of games and quizzes such as crosswords, word searches and hangman.

3.4 Listening Comprehension

Given the voice-only nature of radiotelephony, having good aural comprehension skills becomes critical in the absence of visual clues.

Air-traffic controllers might be able to adhere more easily to ICAO phraseologies when giving clearances but they do ultimately have to comprehend unexpected or unusual messages coming from both professional and non-professional pilots.

We can appreciate the range of language that air-traffic controllers have to contend with by taking a close look at some real live traffic recordings. We can see how even during everyday operations pilots, especially those who are native-English speakers, will have to recourse to plain language expressions. The examples below will also illustrate some of the points mentioned earlier.

*Hello, we've had a **close encounter** with some birds. (= bird strike)*

*There's some **pretty good chop** (= turbulence) here at 140. Do you know how long this is going to **keep up** (= to continue)?*

*We'd like to taxi round **for another go** (= to try/take off again) please.*

*The brakes temperatures are **coming down** (= decreasing), but if we're **in the way** (= obstructing), we can taxi round again using the cooler set of brakes.*

*For information, we just saw a tire roll across the apron in front of us and it's **knocked over** a gate. I know it sounds strange but it might have **fallen off** an aeroplane and just gone across the tarmac.*

In the last two examples the phrasal verbs used would in fact be difficult to replace.

4 Conclusion

The aim of this article has been to demonstrate the relevance of ongoing English language training for air-traffic controllers and the importance of being able to deal effectively with the plain language component of air-traffic communications.

Air-traffic controllers do not necessary have the opportunity to improve their language skills while speaking on the frequency due to the use of phraseology for routine operations. English language training therefore provides the air-traffic controllers with an opportunity to practice and improve their linguistic skills. This might also have a positive effect on stress. The more we understand in foreign language, the lower the stress levels become.

ICAO points out that improvements could be made if native-English speakers also familiarize themselves with the challenges faced by non-native speakers and adopt certain strategies such as:

- Learning strategies to improve cross-cultural communications
- Refraining from the use of idioms, colloquialisms, and other jargon
- Modulating the rate of delivery
- Making sure there is not too much information in a single transmission.

To conclude, ICAO states (ICAO 2004: 1.2.5):

"Although standardized ICAO phraseologies have been developed to cover many circumstances (...), no set of phraseologies can fully describe all possible circumstances and responses. Aircraft are flown and controlled by humans, and human behavior is infinitely invariable; the need to communicate an infinite variety of circumstances or nuances will continue."

Lynette Rees has been working as a regional linguistic coordinator for the French civil aviation authority since 2002. She is in charge of the English language training for the controllers at seven airports in the north east of France and her responsibilities include training and evaluating, harmonizing training programming on a regional and national level and taking part in national working groups. She has also participated in setting up the English language training programs for air traffic controllers in French Polynesia.

References

Eurocontrol (2002): *Safety Regulatory Requirement ESARR 5*, in: http://www.eurocontrol.int/src/public/standard_page/esarr5.html [08.01.2010].

ICAO (International Civil Aviation Organization) (2004): *Manual on the Implementation of ICAO Language Proficiency Requirements*. ICAO Document 9835-AN/453.

ICAO (International Civil Aviation Organization) (2009): *Guidelines for Aviation English Training Programmes*. ICAO Cir 323-AN/185).

http://www.skybrary.aero

Stefan Hinz
Dugald Sturges

ICAO in Military Air Traffic Control
–
First Experiences with a New Language Proficiency Examination

1 Introduction

This article deals with language proficiency examination for military air traffic control (ATC). Although the German Armed Forces are not required by law to adopt the standards and regulations of the International Civil Aviation Organization (ICAO) for their ATC, they do so in the interest of air safety and commissioned the German Federal Office of Languages (Bundessprachenamt, BSprA) with the development of testing procedures.

In section 2, an overview of the development of the ICAO language requirements and their application to testing military ATC is described. The description is followed by a short introduction to the examination procedure (section 3), before giving some first results concerning the performance of the applicants in section 4.

2 The New ICAO Language Requirements

2.1 The History

1997	The ICAO Air Navigation Commission (ANC) reviews the existing provisions for air-ground and ground-ground voice communication in international civil aviation.[1]
2003	The Council of ICAO adopts language Standards and Recommended Practices recommended by the Proficiency Requirements in Common English Study Group (PRICE SG) for pilots, controllers, air traffic service providers and airlines.[2]
2008	These provisions become applicable.[3]
March 2011	Deadline for ICAO member states to ensure that aviation personnel achieve ICAO Level 4 (Operational) proficiency in English.[4]

---

[1] ICAO Resolution A36/11
[2] 32nd Session of the Assembly, September 1998
[3] Language Proficiency Implementation Plan Workshop, Dubai, UAE, 28 to 31 January 2008
[4] http://www.icao.int/fsix/lp/docs/Guidelines.pdf

2.2 The Tasking

In October 2009, the German Air Force Office of Flight Safety (AFSBw) commissions the Federal Office of Languages with the development of regular testing procedures for military Air Traffic Controllers in accordance with ICAO Level 4. In order to obtain a first overview of English language proficiency, all (approx. 300) ATC personnel are administered assessment tests (written 200-point general placement test) by the BSprA in the first half of 2010. In the same year, new testing material in Listening Comprehension and Oral Proficiency is developed in accordance with ICAO Standards in cooperation with the German Armed Forces ATC Office (AFSBw). The development team consists of language specialists from the BSprA, situated in the German Air Force Officer School at Fürstenfeldbruck (Bavaria). The test item approbation is carried out with the help of German Air Force officer candidates and German Federal Police flight school candidates at the Federal Office of Languages.

In December, English language instructors from BSprA at Fürstenfeldbruck and Hürth (near Cologne) and the Army Aviation School in Bückeburg (Lower Saxony) are presented with the new exam and procedures at the Air Force Officer School Fürstenfeldbruck, in particular with the similarities and differences in testing and evaluating English language proficiency according to NATO standard agreement STANAG 6001.[5]

In January 2011, testing in accordance with ICAO Level 4 begins. Test teams initially include 8 examiners from the BSprA, Hürth and its decentralized teaching centers. The exams are carried out predominantly at the three testing venues Hürth, Fürstenfeldbruck and Bückeburg. Whenever possible, the exams take place on location at the respective airfields using mobile testing equipment. Employing both methods allowed for approx. 160 exams to be completed in July 2011. A 2nd round of exams begun in September.

3 Examination Procedure

3.1 Listening Comprehension Test

The test consists of 15 audio items with one multiple choice question per item. Each audio item is heard twice (once for Level 5). 70 % correct answers are required for a pass (11 items).

---

[5] http://www.bilc.forces.gc.ca/stanag/index-eng.asp

3.2 Oral Test

The oral test (see appendix) consists of four parts with

- Part 1: Warm-up, personal introduction. (approx.2 minutes)
- Part 2: Control-related information. Description of job and experience(s). (approx. 2 minutes)
- Part 3: Routine and Non-Routine Situations. Back-to back photo description (aviation situation). (approx. 4 minutes)
- Part 4: Discussion. Aviation safety topics. (approx. 4 minutes)

The Testing Team comprises two language instructors, one Examiner and one Evaluator (with Evaluation Sheet). Test duration is approximately 12 minutes.

4 First Results

After the first round of exams, held at the three test centers and in various locations throughout Germany, it became clear that the vast majority of applicants offer more than a sufficient language proficiency, both in listening comprehension and oral performance, to pass the ICAO Level 4 exam. Pass rates in oral performance are 100 %, in listening they exceed 97 %.

Following an inquiry into the legal necessity of such an examination, it became clear that Armed Forces are not generally required to adopt ICAO regulations for their ATC personnel. Nevertheless, in the interest of aviation safety and ruled by the fact that the military ATC controllers' "realm" reaches well into civil airspace, German military ATC will continue to apply the ICAO language standards to their ATC controllers.

As the German Civil Authorities accept language tests developed and administered by the Federal Office of Languages, a process of combining the regular aviation English preparation course examinations held at the German Officer School is under way. Considerations to raise the testing level to ICAO Proficiency Level 5/6 have led to a review of the testing material pertaining to the respective courses. First results are expected towards the end of 2011.

Stefan Hinz and Dr. Dugald Sturges are members of the Federal Office of Languages (Bundessprachenamt) and tasked with the preparation and administration of ICAO Language Proficiency related examinations within the German Armed Forces.

Appendix: Oral Test Example

2010

GERMAN AIR FORCE
MILITARY AIR TRAFFIC CONTROL
LANGUAGE PROFICIENCY EXAMINATION
for Air Traffic Controllers

ORAL TEST

in compliance with ICAO Language Proficiency Level 4

	MILITARY AIR TRAFFIC CONTROL LANGUAGE PROFICIENCY EXAMINATION ORAL TEST	page 2 2010/03

Part	Description	Time
Part 1	**Personal Introduction**	
Examiner	"My name's .... and this is .... This is the oral part of the recurrent Aviation English Test, based on ICAO Language Proficiency Level 4. I lasts approx. 12 min and contains four parts. Part One is meant to be a warm-up for you to get into speaking English. The actual assessment of your language proficiency will then take place in Parts Two, Three and Four. This assessment lasts 10 min altogether. During the test my colleague will be taking notes about both positive and negative points concerning your speaking skills. If during the test there is something you don't understand, just tell me and I can repeat the question once. Okay? Have you got any questions? Right we will now go on to the first part of the test."	00:00 – 00:30
Q 0	Could you introduce yourself and tell me something about where you come from? *Prompts:* • *When and where did you do your training?* • *Did you receive any additional job training?* • *Where did you take your OJT-training?* • *When did you do your Facility Rating?*	00:30 – 02:00

Part	Description	Time
Part 2	**Control-Related Information**	
Q 1	Could you describe what kind of controlling you do? *Prompts:* • *How long have you been a military ATC controller* • *How long have you been in this position?* • *What do you like about your job?* • *What do you dislike about your job?*	02:00 – 04:00
Q 2	Which military airfield do you work on? *Prompts:* • *Could you describe the airfield for me? Which facilities do they offer?* • *What other airfields have you worked at? Are there any which you would prefer? Why?*	

	MILITARY AIR TRAFFIC CONTROL LANGUAGE PROFICIENCY EXAMINATION ORAL TEST	page 3 2010/03

Part 3	Routine and Non-Routine Situations	
		04:00 – 08:00
Q 3 back-to-back	I would like you to look at the photograph and tell me what you can see. Imagine you have to inform someone else about the situation. Prompts: • Where and when do you think the incident happened? • What could be a possible reason for the incident?	
Q 4	To what extent would an ATC controller be involved in the situation? Prompts: • What has to be done according to the regulations? • Who will be needed to deal with the situation? • Do you consider the surface safe for further operation?	
Q 5	What do you think of the safety standards at GAF aerodromes? Prompts: • Do you think the safety standards are adequately enforced? • What role do the safety briefings play in this respect?	

MILITARY AIR TRAFFIC CONTROL
LANGUAGE PROFICIENCY EXAMINATION
ORAL TEST

Part 4	Discussion	
Q 6	For years, there has been talk about transition in the GAF. What does this mean for you? *Prompts:* • Do you think this will involve modernization of your position? *If YES:* • Could this affect the staff situation? How? • In which way would ATC in general be involved? *If NO:* • When was your workplace modernized the last time? • What was done?	
Q 7	Do you think the budget cuts will have consequences for your work environment? *Prompts:* • What is the present situation at your airfield? • In which way is the job situation affected?	08:00 – 12:00
Q 8	Do you expect your English will improve as a consequence of the new language requirements? Why/ Why not? *Prompts:* • What advice would you give someone who fails to reach Level 4? • Are you satisfied with the language training you received for your job? If not, why?	

End of the Test

Helmut Montag
Martina Sahliger

Incident Investigation or "What Happens when Something has Happened?"

1 Introduction

Regarding the most frequently occurring incidents, it is possible to say that in most cases we have to deal with the phenomenon *Human Factors*. The E DIN IEC 56(Sec)423 defines Human Factors as follows:

> "Human Factors ist eine Disziplin, die sich mit dem Entwurf von Maschinen, Bedienung und Arbeitsumgebung befaßt [...]
> Unter Praktikern wird jede technische Maßnahme zur Berücksichtigung des Faktors Mensch und jede technische Arbeit mit Bezug zum Faktor Mensch als Human Factors bezeichnet [...]
> Die Benennung 'Human Factors' ist austauschbar mit 'human engineering','technische Maßnahmen zur Berücksichtigung des Faktors Mensch' und 'Ergonomie'." (Gröner 2006: 2)

In regard to this definition, we should specify our term and now distinguish between the broad field of Human Factors in general, and the much more specific field of *Human Error* (cf. Dekker 2006: x). This paper will try to explain the investigator's work after an unwelcome incident, dealing with Human Error, rather than the more general term Human Factors.

2 Investigating Persons or Investigating Incidents?

At first glance, it looks like the blame is being put on those persons involved in the examined incidents when talking about Human Error. Dekker calls it "The Old View of Human Error" (Dekker 2006: xi). In his monograph, he points out that everybody who is commissioned to conduct the investigation has to be very careful when talking about the incident. Dekker emphasizes that from his point of view language creates reality. In this case, the use of language reveals that the investigator has put himself outside of what has happened, and this in turn leads to placing the blame on someone instead of finding out what went wrong in the system (Dekker 2006: 46).

2.1 The Retrospective View

In retrospect, Human Error was the "cause of trouble", failure was explained through human incompetence, mistakes and lack of concentration (Dekker 2006: xi). In former days, when risk research was in its early stages, it was the only way an incident was treated. The experts did their research into the causes by looking back and searching for a single reason or even a person to hold responsible for what had happened. On closer inspection, it becomes more and more clear that it is not as easy as it seems.

Meanwhile, it has become obvious that the understanding of an incident depends mainly on how the investigators approach the problem. Are they willing to clarify the circumstances and see the whole picture, or are they content with identifying one single co-factor? Hollnagel stresses in his monograph (2009: 11) that investigators often end their research too early. He calls such behavior the "obeying of the stop-rule". The investigators identify a possible co-factor as the suspected main reason for the incident and do not continue with their work. Thus, the system analysts simply create a new rule to avoid the so-called "reason" for the incident and, after having done their duties everyone goes on in their daily routine as if nothing has happened.

2.2 The Role of "Situational Awareness"

Dekker stresses in his monograph that the "New View of Human Error" focuses on a deeper insight of the system (Dekker 2006: xi). In a similar fashion to Hollnagel, he emphasizes that it is necessary to reconstruct the circumstances which were responsible for the human decisions. One of the main tasks in regard to the circumstances is so-called "situational awareness". Situational awareness is characterized by the cognitive processing of all kind of information, particularly in regard to the actual environment, the technical equipment and instructions. If there are some aspects not detected or not processed, for instance due to language deficiencies, this might lead to uncertainty. Uncertainty, in turn, might lead to a lack of concentration in regard to a special aspect (probably of the flight process). The attention is then focused elsewhere rather than in realizing that the emerging difficult situation may additionally imply an abstract risk.

Another aspect of situational awareness is the idea of different concepts in the understanding of a particular situation. The crew has to perform in a high workload situation. The controller, however, has no clue that the amount of information he gives, without any key words regarding the standard phraseology, is neither heard nor perceived. Thus, the situational concepts do not match, and there is a mishap in understanding and correct assessment of the situation.

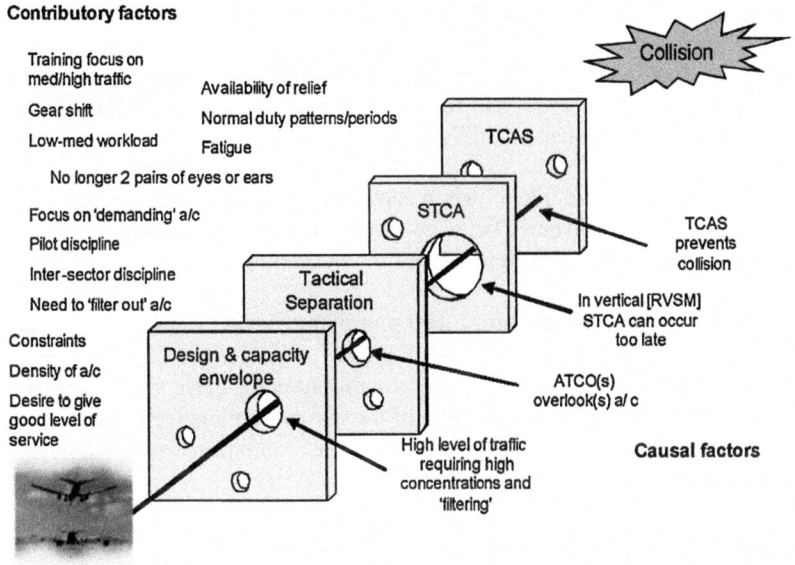

Figure 1: Characterization of the incident pattern
(© Barry Kirwan 2007, in: Hindsight 2007: 13)

Incident investigation is a complex subject. It demands going beyond the so-called obvious reasons to identifying what is called a "bundle" of reasons. Although the graphics may be a few years old, Barry Kirwan's characterization of the incident patterns (see *Figure 1*) is useful for getting an idea of how things can go wrong although they should have gone right (Hollnagel 2009: 97). Although the graphic still symbolizes the retrospective view, it can be seen that there is more than one reason "why things that go right, sometimes go wrong." (Hollnagel 2009: Subtitle). The factors and the co-factors accumulate. The graphic shows a Swiss cheese model, in which almost all holes fit perfectly. The unwanted incident progresses due to the accumulation of contributing factors. In the given example, the separation of two aircraft was not successful; the controller's reaction led to an unpleasant state of affairs and to a deteriorating situation. In the end, the collision was avoided, thanks to TCAS (Traffic Alert and Collision Avoiding System) – the last "slice of cheese" – and these holes did not match (see *Figure 1*).

3 Incident Investigation and Risk Management

Modern incident investigation, therefore, does more than merely look for a culprit. Nowadays it is an important instrument in quality management, integrated mainly into a Safety Management System.

Experts talk about an "incident" when something has gone wrong in the system, for instance when the distance between two aircraft was not as large as it should have been. There are three different types of occurrences:

- *Loss of separation*: the prescribed minimum distance between two aircraft is not kept.
- *Airprox* ("Aircraft Proximity"): Two aircraft come close together where no separation is prescribed, and one of the involved pilots feels at risk.
- *Runway incursion*: An aircraft, a person or a vehicle accesses the safety strip of a runway without clearance.

In which way will these occurrences be investigated? Let us go through an investigation exemplified by an incident called "Loss of Separation".

3.1 An Example: "Loss of Separation"

A loss of separation is a commonly known *low level incident* and is normally reported by the involved controller. In this case the investigator is informed about what happened and when.

After having been alerted, the investigation begins with the collection of all available information on the incident and the backup of the recorded data. It is also very important to get a detailed description of the situation from the participants. The recorded data are the radiotelephony and telephone transmissions, radar data, and when available, the display of the ground movement radar, and finally the flight plan data in written or electronic form. With the help of all these data it is possible to get an idea of how the situation developed.

Loss of separation means that two aircraft came too close together with respect to the prescribed separation minima. The investigator therefore has to analyze the data to answer the question whether the suspected incident really occurred or if the minima were only just abided by. Then he makes use of the radar data and evaluates the distance between the two relevant aircraft.

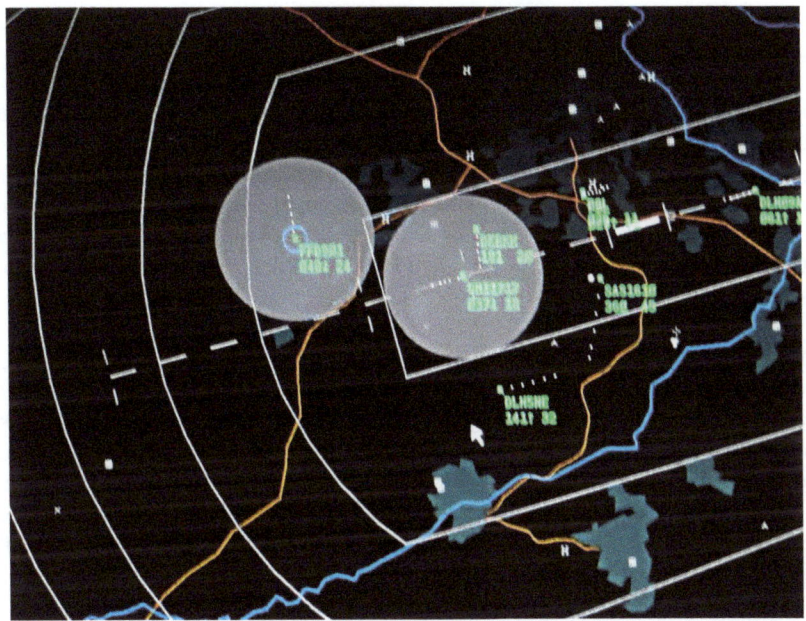

Figure 2: Radar data of two aircraft coming close together
(© Helmut Montag)

The two aircraft in question, shown in *Figure 2*, are not too close together as the circles around the aircraft symbols reveal. These grey circles symbolize the correct distance between the two aircraft on short final. They should not overlap, otherwise a clear loss of separation would have occurred. Here it can be seen that the separation minima are observed and the suspected incident did not occur.

3.2 Prevention Methods and the Persons Involved

The intention of an incident investigation is to find out the weak points in the system rather than to declare someone guilty. Every incident has several aspects. The air traffic control specialist's task is to review the controller's instructions and his communication, particularly the circumstances that led to the incident. In order to go into detail, the help of the involved controller is indispensible. In a confidential interview the ATC specialist and the involved controller talk to each other about what happened from the perspective of the involved controller

(*HERA* – Human Error in ATM[1]). It is a delicate situation, and it demands a high degree of mutual understanding.

Another modern prevention method and an opportunity to get an idea of what could possibly go wrong is the "Voluntary reporting system" (*VRS*[2]). This system allows every pilot and every controller to voluntarily report on what has gone wrong and has not yet been detected, presumably because it was a so-called "low level incident". The person concerned will not be blamed for an incident, but receives assurance that the incident will be looked into in order to reduce abstract risk.

In former days, incidents were examined by just looking back in order to identify a reason for what had happened, so-called retrospection (see section 2.1). Nowadays sociologists suggest changing the direction of view (Dekker 2006; Hollnagel 2009; Renn 2007). Today it is much more important to find out which information had been available to the participants and which decisions had been made using that information. It is a prospective view which includes the whole situation and the whole system. This kind of view offers the opportunity to apply deeper insights regarding the incident for prevention measures.

3.3 Reconstructing Incidents: Transcripts of Communication

Due to the fact that voice communication via radio is the main medium to share information between pilots and controllers, voice recording is the most important data for reconstructing the history of the incident. In order to be able to analyze the data, a transcription of the recordings has to be made with the exact wording and the timing of the communication. Sometimes it is not easy to understand what the communication partners have transmitted, so the investigator has to be very attentive and patient. Sometimes it is necessary to work twenty minutes or more on one single unit in order to identify what has been said until it is clear what the message was all about (cf. Fox this volume). To get a valuable analysis, it is important to focus not only on what has been said but also on how it has been said and furthermore, to pay attention to the time gaps between the controller's instruction and the reply given by the crew.

With these transcripts, an investigator may be able to reconstruct what has been transmitted but not what has been understood. In Pragmatics, this is called the "perlocutive act" (Meibauer 2008; Austin 1975). The speaker has no influence

---

[1] http://www.dfs.de/dfs/internet_2008/module/safety/deutsch/safety/auftrag_sicherheit/human_factors/index.html [01.05.2011]

[2] http://www.dfs.de/dfs/internet_2008/module/safety/deutsch/safety/auftrag_sicherheit/human_factors/index.html [01.05.2011]

on the perception, only the communication partner's reaction reveals whether the transmission was successful or not. A succeeding communication depends not only on the conversational partners but much more on a situation which allows the exchange of information. In order to understand how the incident occurred, it is necessary to keep the whole environment in mind (cf. Sahliger/Renn this volume).

3.3.1 The ICAO Communication Regulations

The International Civil Aviation Organization (ICAO) laid down communication procedures and phrases to keep the difference as small as possible between what has been said and what has been understood. We all know that the ICAO phrases do not cover all possible situations in aviation. Where no regulation exists, the ICAO allows the communication partners the use of plain language. The question is now, how much plain language can be tolerated in a standardized communication before problems arise. Even queries and repetitions will cause a delay to the execution of instructions at a time when the expected reaction should start immediately.

Even when using ICAO phraseology there is an abstract risk of talking at cross purposes. Here, we present the classic example which every controller knows, even though it might only be fiction.

> A pilot is waiting to cross an active runway and asks the tower:
> Pilot: **Tower, request crossing runway zero seven.**
> The Tower answers in a sharp manor, just stating one word:
> Tower: **Negative.**
> (The meaning of the ICAO Phrase "negative" is "no, not allowed", that is "not correct".)
> The Pilot wants to confirm, what he has heard.
> Pilot: **Understand negative.**
> The tower answers again with only one word.
> Tower: **Affirm.**
> (The meaning of the ICAO phrase "affirm" is just "yes")
> The Pilot replies: **Roger, crossing runway zero seven.**

As we see, only ICAO phrases are involved, but nonetheless the result is confusion and misunderstanding. In the given example the pilot asks for permission to cross the runway. The controller denies the permission with only one word: "negative". The pilot asks again, and the controller assumes that the pilot wants to get the confirmation of his refusal. So he answers again with only one word: "affirm". The pilot now refers the controller's second answer, – being opposite to the first one –, to his first question. – And he now assumes having finally got the controller's permission to cross the runway. – To avoid this unwelcome situation, instructions such as "hold short" or "stand by" would have clarified the situation.

From the investigator's perspective, it seems very clear what went wrong in the previous example and how it could have been prevented. Both phrases have to be read back by the crews, they are both unambiguous and for both communication partners certainty of action in terms of operation is guaranteed. – But there are other incidents in which you have to do more to uncover the reason for what happened.

3.3.2 Incident 1: "Follow in Sequence"

In the ears of a controller, the instruction "follow in sequence" does not sound misleading when given to the crew of an aircraft leaving the parking position to taxi to the runway. His intention is to instruct the crew to queue up in a line of aircraft waiting for departure. But sometimes something different happens. The involved controllers are always puzzled as to why the pilots sometimes exceed the instruction and follow the aircraft ahead onto the runway without clearance. This kind of incident is called a "runway incursion". Both pilots in the concerned airplane, captain and co-pilot, stated they had been sure that they had received a line up clearance to enter the runway. How did they come to this conclusion?

As we found out, the keyword is the instruction "follow in sequence". At an airport with more than one runway, one of them may be used in a so-called "single mode". That means that departures will leave on one runway, and arrivals will come in on the other one, and there is no mix-up between them. Pilots of departing aircraft are probably accustomed to hearing the instruction "line up in sequence" to have a continuous flow of departures. Familiar with this phrase, the pilots automatically associate the words "in sequence" with a clearance to enter the runway. The instruction given sounds like an ICAO phrase but it is not one. The correct phrase would be "behind departing line up behind" – a so-called "conditional clearance". The example shows that phrases which are not assigned to a certain situation by definition, as the ICAO phrases are, may have different meanings to different users.

3.3.3 Incident 2: "Wishful Hearing"

While carrying out investigations, another phenomenon can be encountered – the so-called **wishful hearing**. During air traffic control, instructions and clearances are given via radiotelephony. To make sure that the instructions and clearances have been understood in a correct manner the pilots have to repeat the clearance in exactly the same wording, – the so-called "readback". When listening to the voice recording of different incidents, you may recognize very often that the readback was incomplete or wrong – but nobody complained. All participants involved were sure that the given readback was correct. It is the crews' action that makes the difference. Perhaps they probably may have read back incomplete or maybe wrong but have got it right and perform as they should – or maybe they have expected a different instruction and they perform as the expected instruction would have told them. One example may illustrate the situation:

A pilot is used to begin his approach to airport x at FL 100 with a speed of 240 knots in a distance of 37 nm to the threshold of the runway according to the always given instructions by air traffic control. But one morning air traffic control encounters high load traffic and the controller separates the aircraft with the following instruction: "Descend flight level one two zero, reduce speed two hundred knots, fly heading two five zero and contact tower frequency one one niner decimal niner, bye." The crew, being accustomed to hearing "Descend flight level one hundred ...", may probably act as usual. So the aircraft drops below the instructed height. We then talk about an incident called "level bust". Two aircraft have come too close together in the respect of vertical separation. Reason for this incident was wishful hearing, because the crew expected to hear something different as the air traffic controller had really advised.

To understand what was going on, it has to be taken into account under which circumstances the communication between pilots and controllers takes place. For both parties radiotelephony communication is only a part of their work. Pilots have to steer their airplane and are busy with a lot of other tasks in the cockpit. The controller has to plan traffic flow, he is about to prepare the next set of instructions and clearances and will carry out the necessary coordination with other controllers and units.

A reoccurrence of situations is part of the daily routine. Certain instructions will induce a certain reaction and a certain answer, thus the pilots may hear exactly what they expect to hear because that is what they heard during the same situation several times before, although something totally different had been said.

If there is a *keyword* in the transmission, this word can probably create a reaction which was not intended, as illustrated in the following example: The crew of an aircraft, taxiing out for departure, received a transmission from the controller in which he informed the crew about the traffic situation and his further traffic planning. The controller told them: "Two more landings on final, expect departure behind". The crew acknowledged by stating "Jo Jo". The information was not quite necessary, but the controller wanted to give them the reason for a slight delay in departure. What happened? After the first aircraft landed, the aircraft which was about to depart entered the runway and the second one, about to land, was given the instruction to go around. The departing crew was sure that they had received a line up clearance from the responsible controller. Obviously the word "behind", given by the controller during the intended information, was the trigger in this case. Due to a heavy workload in the cockpit, additional distraction probably played a greater part in contributing to this situation. The word "behind" is normally used in connection with the conditional clearance "line up behind" and that was exactly the instruction which the crew expected to hear. If the crew had seen the second aircraft on final, they might have asked the controller and confirmed the supposed line up clearance. But it was a hazy day with the sun shining brightly on a snow covered landscape, and it was very difficult to recognize the incoming aircraft on final approach.

The investigations of special occurrences and incidents reveal that there are always multiple small deficiencies that cumulate and thus contribute to such a situation rather than a single mistake being detected as reason for what happened. Each single contributing factor itself has no effect on the system. It is the accumulation of single events which can contribute to a deterioration of the situation.

4 Conclusion

In order to avoid unwanted outcomes, it seems to be helpful to have a detailed knowledge of the Standard Operating Procedures (SOPs), and furthermore, to have a knowledge of standard phraseologies. However, that is only half the truth. It is also necessary to have an idea about the impact of the deviations from the ICAO standard. Thus, we should focus on the question when it is required to stick to the rules and therefore to adhere exactly to the phraseology, and when it is permitted and even essential to deviate from it. So as to make the right decision in regard to the aforementioned point, it seems to be important for us to acquire a basic knowledge about the cognitive processing of language and communication. Only then will communication partners have the opportunity to think about the necessity of deviation or the maintenance of phraseology. Additionally, it seems to be important that the people concerned have a detailed situational awareness, not only the controllers but also the pilots. The particular situational awareness enables them to evaluate the respective abstract risk.

If an unwelcome incident has nonetheless taken place, it is the investigator's responsibility to identify the factors and co-factors of an unwanted incident for the sake of being able to reduce the abstract risk to a socially accepted level by means of prevention measures.

Martina Sahliger is a linguist (MA) and currently doing her PhD on "radiotelephony in aviation" in Germersheim and Stuttgart. Additionally, she is working as a reader for publishing houses in a media company in Kornwestheim.

Helmut Montag is ATC Specialist at the DFS Tower, site Stuttgart, and active controller TWR/APP. Besides other duties he is responsible for the local safety management in Stuttgart.

References

Austin, John L. (1975): *How to Do Things with Words*. 2nd edition. Cambridge (Massachusetts): Harvard University Press.

Dekker, Sidney (2006): *The Field Guide to Understanding Human Error.* Aldershot: Ashgate.

Gröner, Harald (RWE Power AG): *Human Factors im Arbeitsschutz. Einflüsse menschlicher Faktoren.* Presentation at the TU Bochum on 23rd October 2006.

Hollnagel, Erik (2009): *The ETTO Principle: Efficiency – Thoroughness Trade – Off. Why ThingsThat Go Right Sometimes Go Wrong.* Burlington: Ashgate.

Kirwan, Barry (2007): "Investgating Controller Blind Spots", Hindsight 5, 12-15.

Meibauer, Jörg (2008): *Pragmatik. Eine Einführung,* 2nd edition. Tübingen: Stauffenburg.

Renn, Ortwin (2007): *Risiko. Über den gesellschaftlichen Umgang mit Unsicherheit.* München: oekom.

http://www.dfs.de/dfs/internet_2008/module/safety/deutsch/safety/auftrag_sicherheit/human_factors/index.html [01.05.2011].

Marcel Mattenberger

"Declaring Emergency"
–
A Pilot's View

1 Declaring Emergency?

I have been working as a pilot for over 30 years starting with flying fighter aircraft in the Air force and, later on, airliners in commercial aviation with a total of over 13,000 hours flight time – and I have never declared an emergency.

However, I have spent around 2,000 hours in flight simulators as an instructor and examiner, where pilots are trained in abnormal and emergency situations – and there I hardly attended a simulator session where the crew did not declare an emergency.

What is "Declaring Emergency"?

A few explanations of safety standards and the communication situation in aviation are needed to answer this question.

2 Safety Standards

It is common knowledge that the safety standards in aviation are very high and sufficiently devised. I would like to exemplify the safety system on the *MD11*, a three-engine long-haul aircraft, which has the capacity to fly non-stop 12-hour flights with about 250 passengers (the distance flown is equal to almost a quarter of the circumference of the earth).

2.1 "One System only"

Aircraft such as the MD11, the Airbus or the Boeing aircraft are all designed in the same way: every technical system exists either twice or even three times (e.g., three engines or three communication devices). Whenever one of the systems fails, the pilots can rely on the remaining system. When the system is of high importance it exists in triplicate, in order to have a backup of the backup, e.g., for air data such as speed and altitude. That way the indications can still be cross-checked.

Should a crew fall back on only one system, they consider this situation an emergency and have to act accordingly, which in most cases means an immediate landing. They then "Declare Emergency" to alert ground control and other aircraft, so that they know an aircraft is in an exceptional situation and needs special attention, like priority in communication or landing.

2.2 An Example: the MD11

Applying the above-mentioned principles to the MD11, we get the following scenarios:

- When one of three engines fails, the cockpit crew is not yet in a state of emergency: they still have two running engines (many other aircraft only have a total of two!). The cockpit crew faces a real emergency should the second engine fail.
- A commercial aircraft is always flown by two pilots; should one of them become incapable of action – for example through food poisoning[1] – the other pilot finds himself in an emergency situation: he has to fly the aircraft alone and therefore will have to land immediately.
- The aircraft is designed to reach its final destination after a twelve-hour flight. Nevertheless, it has enough fuel on board to reach an alternate airport. If an airport closes due to weather conditions or because of an accident, the crew has to be able to reach an alternate airport that is suitable for the landing of an aircraft of the same size. Should the cockpit crew, in the course of the flight, realize that they do not have enough fuel to fulfill this condition, they are close to facing an emergency: if they proceed without doing anything, they have only one landing possibility – thus they fall back to "*one system only*". To avoid such an emergency situation, they will usually plan an intermediate landing to get sufficient fuel to reach the destination and, additionally, to have the required amount of remaining fuel for the alternate airport.

As one can see, there are a number of regulations that aim at covering, or avoiding all possible emergency situations. A crucial point here is *communication*, especially communication between the cockpit crew and ground control. In the following passage we will take a more detailed look at the difficult conditions of communication in commercial aviation, and the resulting problems and regulations.

---

[1] The same safety standard applies even to the question of what to choose from the menu: a pilot always eats a different dish than the one his co-pilot picked.

3 Communication in Commercial Aviation

As mentioned above, commercial aircraft for flights within Europe or long-haul flights are usually equipped with three radios. For long-distance communication there is additional radio equipment, and with new technologies there are means of data transfer in written form. Not only that, but the ground station presents a similar picture: the ATC (Air Traffic Control) controller has to have the same technical equipment as the aircraft. This is the case in Europe and many other regions in the world, but not necessarily everywhere.

3.1 Challenging Conditions: Equipment and Amount of Traffic

First of all, the conditions for transmitting a spoken message are basically still the same as more than 100 years ago – the time when this method of communication was discovered (among others by Marconi, an Italian physicist; cf. Skolnik 2008). Transmission through radio waves is a physical process and is therefore bound to certain "natural" rules. It has, for example, a limited range. The communication method used today (*very high frequency, VHF*) has a maximum range of about 250 NM^2 or 450 km. Other means (*high frequency, HF*) have a broader range, but they are of bad or sometimes even very bad quality.

In future, more use will certainly be made of electronic data transfer, but not all communication can be done in written form: as soon as a directive is communicated that has to be followed by the crew immediately, radio communication becomes the only possible communication method. Imagine an aircraft approaching Frankfurt airport; the ATC controller leads one aircraft after the other to the extended center line of the landing runway in a 3 to 5 NM sequence, and the crew has to acknowledge and follow the order without time delay – a task that cannot be accomplished in written form. To manage the huge amount of air traffic in the vicinity of a busy airport, speed in communication is mandatory and "writing letters" does not suffice in this situation.

This is the daily environment cockpit crews and ATC controllers have to work in – and, above all, have to work in together. Sometimes a permanent flow of orders, questions, answers and acknowledgments is "in the air". Both parties have to pay close attention to recognize when they are addressed, act accordingly and,

---

[2] Nautical Mile, one nautical mile equals 1,852 meters.

in the meantime, listen to the exchange of information concerning aircraft in their vicinity, which might affect them and their actions as well.[3]

3.2 Understanding the Others

Besides the technical aspects interfering with the quality of communication, there are also certain "human factors". These contribute to an even greater extent to the problems in aviation communication. Some problems which arise in this context are:

- A crew does not hear that the controller's message is directed at them.
- There are two transmissions at the same time. A situation which arises quite often, as nobody knows when another party is starting to talk. Two transmissions at the same time at the same radio-frequency result in a garbled noise, which is not understandable.
- People in the cockpit or in the control center are distracted because of other persons or incidents.
- A pilot or a controller has his/her own way to communicate, e.g. uses 'funny' terms to express his intelligence.
- A person has a very strong accent, e.g. German, French or Asian.
- Somebody does not have a sufficient command of English.
- Orders are not understood or misinterpreted, because the person they are directed at does not know the procedures of an airport.
- Two parties simply do not understand each other.

How can these deficiencies be counteracted? One important means is a standard phraseology that has been developed by the aviation community with its different bodies (ICAO[4], IATA[5], EASA[6], state authorities, etc.). Pilots and controllers have to follow a small set of rules (cf. ICAO 2007):

- Use "aviation English".
- Always read back (i.e., repeat) an instruction.
- As a controller, listen to the read back to double check correct understanding.

---

[3] To get an impression of authentic air traffic communication, you can listen to the live transmission of the ATC control of a major airport on the internet, e.g. at http://www.liveatc.net/.
[4] International Civil Aviation Organization (http://www.icao.int/)
[5] International Air Transport Association (http://www.iata.org/Pages/default.aspx)
[6] European Aviation Safety Agency (http://www.easa.eu.int/)

- If somebody has not understood a message or is insecure if he/she has correctly understood: ask for a "say again".

In Europe, most participants follow these standards in a more or less consistent manner, but nevertheless communication problems are not unusual. For example, if the communicating parties' mother tongue is English, they might fall back into a "conversational style", which can be hard to understand for non-native listeners. In the U.S., I witnessed a situation where a native English controller showered a non-native cockpit crew member with instructions and was asked to "say again". He then repeated the same orders with the same words and speed, just with a slightly louder voice. Only the subsequent additional request "say it again – slowly!" made him realize the real cause of the communication problem.

This example and many other similar incidents reveal not only the origins of many communication problems, but also two important means to overcome these problems: *conscientiousness* and *discipline*, the first one emphasizing the importance of a correctly applied standard phraseology, the second one relating to the use of this phraseology.

4 Communication as a Source of Emergency Situations?

Talking as a pilot about communication in aviation I can not only focus on the exchange of information. The situation, in which the communication takes place, has always to be considered as well. In this perspective and in the understanding of the pilot, flying the aircraft is the main task for the pilot. Communication helps to fulfill this task. Most operators have developed programs to focus on the importance of working together between cockpit crew and ATC controllers for the improvement of aviation safety.-Workshops take place with participants from "both sides", the "cockpit" and the "control tower". These workshops improve the mutual understanding of the specific problems of each group of participants and aim at a better cooperation and more safety in everyday aviation communication.

After having outlined the daily communication life of cockpit crews and ATC controllers I would like to come back to the question you might ask:

Is there a situation in communication where a cockpit crew (or a controller) has to "Declare Emergency"?

There should be no such situation, if the principles I described are adhered to by all participants. The only situation in which an emergency in communication has to be declared is the total failure of the communication equipment in the aircraft or on the ground. The odd thing about this situation (total technical communication failure) is that you are not able to transmit or to receive the emergency message because all your radios are dead.

It would not be aviation if there did not exist, even for this situation, a backup, namely the radio failure procedures cockpit crews have to follow in such a situation. The ATC controller knows what the cockpit crew has to do and will do. Therefore both sides, the ATC controller and the crew (hopefully) will, once again, act in complete coordination for the sake of safety.

As we try so hard and have competent, disciplined and conscientious people at our disposal, we should not have to face an emergency situation in communication. There is no need for a "Declaring *Communication* Emergency"!

Marcel Mattenberger, 58, was working as an instructor, examiner and pilot (with over 13,000 flight hours) for over 30 years on short and long haul aircraft for Swissair and Swiss International Airlines. Now retired.

References

Skolnik, Merrill I. (2008): *Radar Handbook*, 3rd edition. New York: The McGraw-Hill Companies.

ICAO (International Civil Aviation Organization) (2007): *Manual of Radiotelephony*, 4th edition. ICAO Document 9432-AN/925.

Martina Sahliger
Ortwin Renn

Communication Needs in a High Risk Environment

1 Introduction

The fast development of the airline industries during the last decades caused increasing requirements by the public, customers and politics concerning technical safety and international security. A highly differentiated and complex system of laws and regulations exist on the regional, national, and international level. Airline Companies all over the world have to comply with a multitude of laws and regulations, which in part conflict with each other.

In addition to the legal requirements, airline corporations face increasing demands for more information and participation to their customers, special stakeholder groups, and the public at large. The need for improved risk and safety communication has been voiced since the late 1960s. This request for more information and communication was mainly directed towards the interactions between airline industry spokespersons and the outside world, in particular customers, regulators and NGOs. However, as recent studies show (Löfstedt 2003; Hertel/Henseler 2007), the communication within the organization is often even more important for the overall safety record than the communication to the outside world.

The ultimate goal of risk communication is to assist stakeholders and the public at large in understanding the rationale of a risk-based (risk-informed) decision, and to arrive at a balanced conclusion that reflects the factual evidence of the matter at hand in relation to their own interests and values (Aven/Renn 2010). In other words, good practices in risk communication are meant to help all affected parties make informed choices about matters that are of concern to them. It is the purpose of risk communication to provide people with all the insights they need in order to make decisions or judgments that reflect the best available knowledge and their own preferences. This is true for professional as well as lay audiences.

This paper will deal with the communication among professionals. It will address the highly formalized interactions between pilots and air traffic controllers. Section 2 provides an introduction to professional risk communication and its functions. Section 3 is primarily concerned with communication and understanding in high stress situations, regarded from a linguistic point of view. The conclusions reached in the two chapters bring both perspectives together (see section 4).

2 Three Levels of Risk Communication

One of the major goals of all risk communication programs is to reconcile the legitimate intention of the communicator to get a message across with the equally legitimate set of concerns and perceptions that each person associates with the risk agent (Aven/Renn 2010). It is obvious that technical experts try to communicate the extent of their expertise while their communicative counterparts may be more interested in potential impacts of their common actions. Regardless of the intention of the communicator, the first step in any communication effort is to find a common denominator, a common language, in which the communication can proceed and develop. In spite of the fact that controller and pilots pursue the same overall goal (safe landing of an airplane), they have different language cultures and different ways of articulating their messages. This will be further developed from a linguistic perspective in section 3.

Finding a common denominator or "being on the same page" requires a good understanding of the audience's needs. Having investigated many different types of audiences and issues, our own research has led us to a classification of typical communication levels that are normally addressed during a risk debate (based on Funtowicz/Ravetz 1985; first published in Renn/Levine 1991; refinement in Aven/Renn 2010). These levels refer to:

- factual evidence and probabilities;
- institutional performance, expertise, and experience;
- conflicts about world views and value systems.

Figure 1 is a graphical representation of this model using a modified version of the original categories. The first level involves technical information and formal procedures. The function of communication on the first level is to provide the most accurate picture of the situation, including the treatment of uncertainties. Even if the objective here is create a common understanding of the problem, an attempt at two-way communication is needed to ensure that the message has been understood and that all open questions have been addressed. As will be shown later this is less than easy, particularly in an environment in which the language of communication is not the native language of those who interact with each other. Furthermore, the routine of using always the same terms is difficult to sustain so that ambiguities might be added just for the sake of variability.

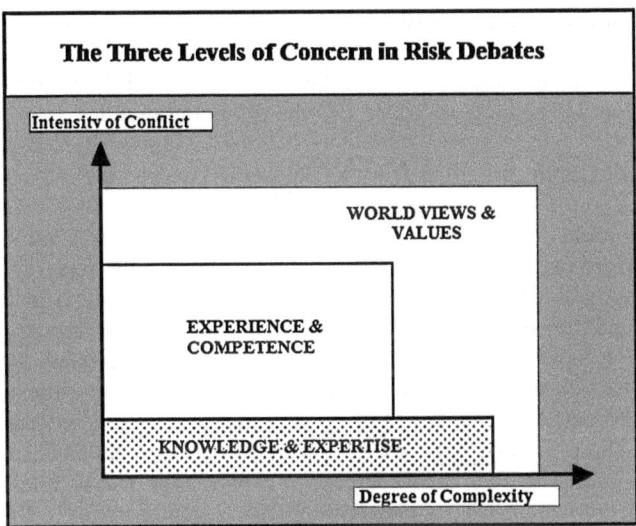

Figure 1: Levels of concern in risk debates (adapted from Renn/Levine 1991)

The second, more intense, level of debate is concerned with institutional competence of dealing with the risks. At this level, the focus of the debate is on the trustworthiness of the risk management institutions. This type of debate does not rely on technical expertise, although reducing scientific uncertainty may help. In the case of the communication between pilot and controller it is essential that both parties trust each other and have confidence that the messages exchanged will lead to the required actions. Such trust relationship is not always given, in particular if pilots come from other cultures or countries that are deemed as less reliable as the home country of the controller. It is essential, particularly in high risk situations, to rely on competence and expertise.

At the third level, the conflict is defined by different social values and cultural lifestyles, and their impact upon risk management. In this case, neither technical expertise nor institutional competence and openness are adequate conditions for risk communication. Dealing with values and lifestyles requires a fundamental understanding of the issues that are subject to the risk debate. This implies that the communication requirements of the first and second level (i.e. risk information or involvement in a two-way dialogue) can not suffice in finding a solution that is acceptable to all or most parties. Third-level debates are rare in the communication between pilots and controllers. They could, however, be relevant if specific terms that deviate from the formal language have different meanings in different cultures.

Debates on all three levels of risk communication rely on basic understanding of messages between sender and receiver. Without a proper understanding of each other, none of the functions on each of the levels can be fulfilled. The basic ideas of linguistic understanding are covered in the following sections.

3   High Risk Communication from a Linguistic Perspective

Medicine, nuclear technology, and aviation have one thing in common: society has to rely on the knowledge and the trustworthiness of those who are experts of these technologies. During a flight or during a stay in a hospital the individual person depends on the performance and skills of those who are in charge for their safety. A small error of the responsible persons will probably have a great impact on the safety of the concerned person, not to mention on the system (i.e. aviation), particularly if one has to deal with a tightly coupled and complex system where there is only little or no space for errors and mistakes (Perrow 1984: 5). That is why such technologies are called "high risk technologies" and this kind of communication is called "high risk communication". Communication in high risk technologies has to meet the demand of being unambiguous. Misleading communication and ambiguities can cause misunderstanding and therefore lead to severe mistakes, which can endanger human life, particularly when the communication language is not the mother tongue of the interacting persons.

3.1   Second Language Acquisition and Learning Strategies – Language for Special Purposes in a Foreign Language

Languages for special purposes are generally based on a natural language. In regard of aviation the ICAO (International Civil Aviation Organization) has decided that it is necessary to establish a common way of sufficient communication all over the world. The English language should be the medium of correspondence and audio-verbal communication. Thus most participants in aviation have to acquire the standard language in aviation during second language acquisition.

Depending on the research field there are several theories concerning first language acquisition. The most known theory in linguistics has been developed by Noam Chomsky. He assumed that there might exist an internal system which is responsible for developing the mother tongue. For him first language acquisition is some kind of "ripening process" rather than a real "learning process". Chomsky stated that a baby gets much too few data during its first three years of life for being able to develop the grammar only by analyzing the spoken words. So the question arose how language is represented in the brain and how it gets in. Chomsky claimed that it might probably perform as some kind of "switches" which have to be set for activating the correct grammar, the correct spelling and the correct set of phonemes. This *internal system* is active until the little human has acquired his or her mother tongue. After the mother tongue has been developed completely, the internal system expires (Chomsky 1969: 81, 1981: 107), and from that moment on different strategies are needed to acquire a foreign language. Chomsky claims an *external system* which starts to be active after the internal system has expired and helps us now to acquire a foreign language – as we all know, more or less successful. There are several theories how this might come to be, and there is strong evidence that the most successful strategy in acquiring a foreign language is the acquisition of a second language with the help of phraseologies (Aguado 2002: 27; cf. also Šimunek 2007). Sentences that are often heard, songs and phrasal verbs are stored in the brain. These phraseologies are the basis of the vocabulary and also of the successful extraction of the grammatical structure regarding the language to be learnt (Aguado 2002: 27).

Particularly Aviation English is based on the phraseologies created by the ICAO for the purpose of communication between the controllers and the crews. To be able to communicate in Aviation English, non-native speakers have to attend several classes where ICAO phraseologies are the subject of education. Depending on which certificate is to be attained, there are several flight simulations that need to be completed, not only in order to acquire the particular vocabulary but moreover to get an idea about the techniques, the Standard Operating Procedures (SOPs) and the features of airports and General Aviation, and furthermore, about the particularities of airline piloting.

3.2 Production and Comprehension of Utterances

It is therefore essential that the communication process in this kind of technology is unambiguous and clearly understandable. During radiotelephony the conversational partners communicate in Aviation English. Sometimes radio contact is bad due to interference and a high amount of traffic. Thus, it is important to get the message across, whether by phraseologies or whether by colloquial language. The Federal Aviation Administration (FAA) emphasizes in its publications: "Since concise phraseology may not always be adequate, use whatever words are necessary to get your message across" (FAA 2010, chapter 4-2-1).

There are several demands on the production of speech (ICAO 2007: 15). Certain linguistic features are responsible for the ability to perceive a message and perform accordingly:

- Articulation: it is important to speak clearly, with a normal voice and without a deforming accent. The listener should be able to identify the uttered words without any problems.
- Intonation: the stress of the words should correctly be emphasized. It might be irritating when it differs from the normal routine.
- Prosody: not all utterances have the same prosody. A question has a different intonation than an advice or even than a statement. The comprehension process will be prolonged if the prosody differs too much from the intended utterance.
- Syntax: the communication should contain short and correctly constructed sentences. Generally, they are provided by the ICAO phraseology.
- Semantics: every word has got its own particular meaning. However, a term has a different range of meanings than its colloquial counterpart. So it is necessary to know exactly on which kind of conversational level the communication is based. In high risk environments there is no space for interpretations. Special language is defined – colloquial language has to be interpreted.
- Sometimes it is necessary to deviate from the ICAO standard to inform the conversational partner about a particular situation, because not all imaginable situations are covered by the ICAO phraseology. Then the speaker has no other choice than to make use of plain language (cf. Rees this volume). A speaker who is unfamiliar with the target language faces the difficulty of making an utterance in the foreign language in such a way that the original intention can still be recognized, particularly if there is no adequate linguistic concept available in the target language.
- Speech rate: the ICAO Manual of Radiotelephony recommends a speech rate "not exceeding 100 words per minute" (ICAO 2007: 15). However, recorded data reveals that a large percentage of speakers follow a speech rate twice or three times faster than recommended due to a high work load (cf. Bieswanger this volume). In any case it is a rather inaccurate value. Given the fact that some words have three or more syllables, it is difficult to compare them with words with only one syllable. A word with more than one syllable takes more time to speak than a word formed with only one syllable. Thus, this leads to the conclusion that the correct speech rate is much higher than assumed.

3.3 Linguistic Factors Contributing to a Successful Communication

Additionally, we have to cope with the fact, that every communication process is embedded in a particular situation. Communication itself is seen as a kind of behavior – "linguistic behavior" (Linke 2001: 173). This has a great impact on the comprehension process. Every uttered sentence has a particular intention (*illocutionary act*), is uttered within a specific situation and will be perceived by the listener in a *perlocutionary act*. All these three elements are part of a so-called "speech act", first developed by Austin in 1955. The perlocutionary act, however, cannot be influenced by the speaker; it is the moment when the sound arrives at the listener's ear and the comprehension process begins. Möhle describes an utterance as "Nach-Außen-Bringen, ein Externalisieren von gedanklichen Tatbeständen oder Zusammenhängen mit den Mitteln der Sprache" (Möhle 1997: 40).

According to Möhle, a linguistic utterance is based on a "cognitive concept" (Möhle 1997: 43) expressed by a particular term being verbalized during the speech act. Searle stresses that there is no linguistic utterance during conversation without a speaker's particular intention (Searle 1971: 38). Even a simple greeting such as "Good morning" is uttered with the intention of being polite and making the conversational partner comfortable.

Linguistic behavior during a conversation is important for communication in high risk environments. During ATC Communication (ATC = Air Traffic Control) controllers steer an aircraft only by the power of their words. That means that every piece of advice is a particular speech act. The pilot has to execute the controller's advice immediately, no matter whether he likes it or not. Only compelling reasons for not being able to perform are accepted by air traffic control.

The listener has to understand what has been said. Therefore, we not only have to deal with the simple physical facts of phonetics but moreover with the perlocutionary act where the speaker, after having finished his message, has no influence on the comprehension process (Searle 1971: 42). It is a moment of uncertainty until the listener signalizes his agreement. That means that the speaker might have had a particular idea, but, unfortunately, the listener did not understand it correctly. He might have misunderstood the message because the utterance was not understandable or ambiguous or because the "chemistry is wrong" between the two conversational partners. This means that the communication process is "out of control".

There are several aspects which contribute to successful communication. Both communication partners are included in a particular situation which might be defined, such as the communication during an instrumental flight. Generally this form of conversation occurs while steering an aircraft either by the crew or through the controller's words. Conversation should strictly be limited to the advice and the expected answers; "chatting" is not intended by the official organizations. Comprehension of an utterance depends on correct semantic *coding* and *decoding*. Regarding the *situation*, it can be said that the crew and the controller have almost the same knowledge of what and how it has to be done. Thus there seem to be no surprises during the daily routine. Phraseology, called "frame" (Koll-Stobbe 1997: 53), is to be uttered in a particular context, called "scene" (Koll-Stobbe 1997: 52) within a defined situation. The empirical knowledge and the particular linguistic knowledge of both conversational partners, even though it does not always coincide, contribute to this situation (Linke 2001: 175). Furthermore, it is a "remote" communication. The conversational partners are far away from each other, the controllers mostly sit in so-called "control centers" and the crew, up in the air, all have to rely on microphones. Thus the aircraft is only a flashing little green spot on a black screen, moving slowly from one sector to another. No matter how difficult such conversations might be, they have to be conducted successfully every day and anywhere in the world. It is therefore important to make the utterances as short as possible but as extensive as necessary.

Successful communication also depends on the *conversational maxims*, developed from the "felicity conditions" created by Austin (1975: 14) and redefined by Grice in 1989. In pragmatics, the conversational maxims play an important role. A speaker can stick to them or can violate them. Violated conversational maxims sometimes lead to irony or indirectly – and therefore very polite – uttered requests such as: "Didn't you want to get up early tomorrow morning?" during an intensive discussion among friends late on a Sunday evening.

What are the conversational maxims?

- Maxim of quality: Make your contribution one that is true.
- Maxim of quantity: Make your contribution as informative as is required. Do not make your contribution more informative than is required.
- Maxim of relevance: Be relevant.
- Maxim of manner: Be perspicuous, avoid obscurity of expression, avoid ambiguities, be brief, be orderly (Meibauer 2008: 25).

Undoubtedly, 99 % of the aviation conversation is successful. Asked about the reasons for that, some sociologists would answer that there were the circumstances leading to a satisfying exchange. The linguists would probably like to add that the conversational partners fulfilled the conditions described by the conversational maxims.

During high risk communication it is necessary to follow these rules to achieve an unambiguous conversation. Irony and ambiguity are not wanted during radiotelephony contact; the risks of misunderstandings and mistakes are too high. Furthermore, in many cases during radiotelephony contact at least one conversational partner is a non-native-speaker of the English language. Without the use of phraseology, problems might occur while trying to get the intended message across. Möhle stresses the difficulties of expressing an utterance in a foreign language in such a way that the intended message is perceived, although there is a lack of adequate concepts in the target language (1997: 43). The speaker is then forced to paraphrase and he has to look for an expression which is close to the concepts of the target language but might not fit completely. To do so successfully means that the speaker has to speak the target language fluently. It has, however, been observed that the utterances of a non-native-speaker in a target language are highly influenced by the syntax and semantics of his / her own mother tongue (Möhle 1997: 44). And as a consequence, syntax and vocabulary mistakes occur all too commonly.

Thus, communication in high risk environments has to be performed in such a way that misunderstandings are reduced to a minimum and utterances have to be made as unambiguous as possible. Deviations from ICAO Standard can therefore lead to misunderstandings or to non-comprehension because something completely different had been expected by the conversational partner.

4 Conclusion

The main message of this paper is that *risk communication goes beyond the act of exchanging messages*. It needs to be seen as a complex activity of mutual interactions and sharing a sense of common understanding. Sending out messages is insufficient in overcoming the problems of assuring exact understanding in high risk situations and to make cooperative behavior function as planned (Bohnenblust/Slovic 1998). The potential remedies to these two problems lie in a *better language performance* and in structuring the risk communication program mainly as a *process of exchanging well-defined signals that are unambiguous and directly related to significant action*. Careful management oversight, excellent training of personnel, commitment to agreed-upon standards of interaction and continuous effort to improve one's performance are important conditions for being successful in high risk communication. These conditions cannot guarantee success, but they make it more probable.

The second most important message is that risk management and risk communication should be seen as parallel activities that complement each other. Risk communication supports ongoing management and safety efforts. By carefully reviewing in-house performance, by tailoring the content of the communication to the needs of the receivers, and by adjusting the messages to the situation and the task, risk communication can meet its predefined task and thus, over time, create the foundations for a trustworthy relationship between the communicator and the target audience (Renn 1992).

The third main message is to take differences in semantic perception seriously. Any successful risk communication program needs to address the problems faced by the variability of assigning meaning to identical words or phrases. This is particularly problematic if the speaker and the receiver have different native languages. Language perception studies can help to anticipate likely reactions to known or unknown phrases.

The fourth main message is that in situations of high stress and strict social rules for a standardized communication routine, communicators have a hard time to stick to the agreed-upon terms and phrases. Our empirical research has shown that controllers start to change words and phrases after 20-30 minutes. It is obviously extremely difficult to repeat the exact same phrases over and over again in a situation where all other tasks demand high awareness and professional handling of difficult situations. This discrepancy between boring repetition of phrases and high alert may lead to cognitive dissonance (Festinger 1957) that can be resolved either by changing phrases or shifting to a routine performance mode. Both responses are suboptimal with respect to airline safety. How to address this problem is not quite clear. One might think of shorter intervals between work and breaks or by installing word recorders that blink or change color if a word outside of the formal language is chosen.

Ortwin Renn serves as full professor and Chair of Environmental Sociology and Technology Assessment at Stuttgart University (Germany). He directs the Interdisciplinary Research Unit for Risk Governance and Sustainable Technology Development (ZIRN) at Stuttgart University and the non-profit company DIALOGIK, a research institute for the investigation of communication and participation processes in environmental policy making.

Martina Sahliger is a linguist (MA) and currently doing her PhD on "radiotelephony in aviation" in Germersheim and Stuttgart. Additionally she is working as a reader for publishing houses in a media company in Kornwestheim.

References

Aguado, Karin (2002): "Formelhafte Sequenzen und ihre Funktion für den L2-Erwerb", *Zeitschrift für Angewandte Linguistik* 37.2, 27-49.

Austin, John L. (1975): *How to Do Things with Words*, 2nd edition. Cambridge (Massachusetts): Harvard University Press.

Aven, Terje/Ortwin Renn (2010): *Risk Management*. Heidelberg/New York: Springer.

Bahns, Jens/Hartmut Burmester/Thomas Vogel (1986): "The Pragmatics of Formulae in L2 Learner Speech: Use and Developments", *Journal of Pragmatics* 10.6, 693-723.

Hertel, Rolf F./Gernot Henseler (ed.) (2007): *ERiK-Development of a Multi-Stage Risk Communication Process*. Berlin: Bundesinstitut für Risikobewertung (Federal Institute for Risk Assessment).

Börner, Wolfgang/Klaus Vogel (ed.) (1997): *Kognitive Linguistik und Fremdspracherwerb. Das mentale Lexikon*. Tübingen: Narr.

Bohnenblust, Hans/Paul Slovic (1998): "Integrating Technical Analysis and Public Values in Risk-Based Decision Making", *Reliability Engineering and System Safety* 59.1, 151-159.

Chomsky, Noam (1969): *Aspekte der Syntax-Theorie*. Frankfurt a.M.: Suhrkamp.

Chomsky, Noam (1981): *Regeln und Repräsentationen*. Frankfurt a.M.: Suhrkamp.

Coulmas, Florian (1979): "On the Sociolinguistic Relevance of Routine Formulae", *Journal of Pragmatics* 3.3-4, 239-266.

Dietrich, Rainer (2003): *Communication in High Risk Environments*. Hamburg: Buske.

Dietrich Rainer/Kateri Jochum (2004): *Teaming Up: Components of Safety under High Risk*. Aldershot: Ashgate.

FAA (Federal Aviation Administration) (2010): *Aeronautical Information Manual. Official Guide to Basic Flight Information and ATC Procedures*. US Department of Transportation. http://www.faa.gov/air_traffic/ publications/ATPubs/AIM/aim.pdf

Festinger, Leo (1957): *A Theory of Cognitive Dissonance*. Stanford: Stanford University Press.

Funtowicz, Silvio O./Jeromy R. Ravetz (1985): "Three Types of Risk Assessment Methodological Analysis", in: Whipple, Chris/Vincent Covello (ed.): *Risk Analysis in the Private Sector*. New York: Plenum Press.

ICAO (International Civil Aviation Organization) (2007): *Manual of Radiotelephony*, 4th edition. ICAO Document 9432-AN/925.

Koll-Stobbe, Amei (1997): "Verstehen von Bedeutungen: Situative Wortbildungen und mentales Lexikon", in: Börner, Wolfgang/Klaus Vogel (ed.): *Kognitive Linguistik und Fremdsprachenerwerb. Das mentale Lexikon*, 2nd revised edition. Tübingen: Narr.

Linke, Angelika et al. (2001): *Studienbuch Linguistik*, 4th edition. Tübingen: Niemeyer.

Löfstedt, Ragnar (2003): "Risk Communication Pitfalls and Promises", *European Review* 11.3, 417-435.

Meibauer, Jörg (2008): *Pragmatik. Eine Einführung*, 2nd revised edition. Tübingen: Stauffenburg.

Möhle, Dorothea (1997): "Deklaratives und prozedurales Wissen in der Repräsentation des mentalen Lexikons", in: Börner, Wolfgang/Klaus Vogel (ed.): *Kognitive Linguistik und Fremdsprachenerwerb. Das mentale Lexikon*, 2nd revised edition. Tübingen: Narr.

Morgan, Morgan/Baruch Fischhoff/Ann Bostrom/Cynthia J. Atman (2001): *Risk Communication: A Mental Models Approach*. Cambridge: Cambridge University Press.

Perrow, Charles (1984): *Normal Accidents. Living with High-Risk Technologies*. Princeton: Princeton University Press.

Renn, Ortwin (1992): "Risk Communication: Towards a Rational Dialogue with the Public", *Journal of Hazardous Materials* 29.3, 465-519.

Renn, Ortwin/Deborah Levine (1991): "Credibility and Trust in Risk Communication", in: Kasperson, Roger/Piet J. Stallen (ed.): *Communicating Risk to the Public*. Dordrecht: Kluwer Academic Publishers, 175-218.

Rohrmann, Bernd/Ortwin Renn (2000): "Risk Perception Research: An Introduction", in: Renn, Ortwin/Bernd Rohrmann (ed.): *Cross-Cultural Risk Perception: A Survey of Empirical Studies*. Dordrecht/Boston: Kluwer, 11-54.

Schwarz, Monika (2008): *Einführung in die Kognitive Linguistik*. Tübingen/Basel: Francke.

Searle, John R. (1971): *Sprechakte*. Frankfurt a M.: Suhrkamp.

Šimunek, Robert (2007): *Formelhafte Sprache und Internetprojekte*. Tübingen: Narr.

FTSK
Publikationen des Fachbereichs Translations-, Sprach- und Kulturwissenschaft der Johannes Gutenberg-Universität Mainz in Germersheim

REIHE A - Abhandlungen und Sammelbände

Band 1 Dietrich Briesemeister (Hrsg.): Sprache, Literatur, Kultur. Romanistische Beiträge. 1974.

Band 2 Reinhart Herzog (Hrsg.): Computer in der Übersetzungswissenschaft. Sprachpraktische und terminologische Studien. 1981.

Band 3 Karl-Heinz Stoll: The New British Drama. A Bibliography with Particular Reference to Arden, Bond, Osborne, Pinter, Wesker. 1975.

Band 4 Sergej Mawrizki: Außenhandel der Sowjetunion gestern und heute. Grundlagen, Entwicklung und der Westhandel nach dem Zweiten Weltkrieg. 1976.

Band 5 Michael T. Trabert: Das religiöse Erbe im Frühwerk Philip Roths. *Goodbye Columbus*. 1985.

Band 6 H. W. Drescher / Signe Scheffzek (Hrsg.): Theorie und Praxis des Übersetzens und Dolmetschens. 1976. (vergriffen)

Band 7 Dagmar Steffen: Der Zweiakter im zeitgenössischen englischen Drama. Studien zu John Mortimers *The Judge,* David Mercers *After Haggerty* und *Flint* und Tom Stoppards *Jumpers.* 1983.

Band 8 J. Albrecht / H. W. Drescher / H. Göhring / N. Salnikow (Hrsg.): Translation und interkulturelle Kommunikation. 40 Jahre Fachbereich Angewandte Sprachwissenschaft der Johannes Gutenberg-Universität Mainz in Germersheim. 1987. (vergriffen)

Band 9 Renate von Bardeleben (Hrsg.): Wege amerikanischer Kultur / Ways and Byways of American Culture. Aufsätze zu Ehren von / Essays in Honor of Gustav H. Blanke. 1989.

Band 10 Christel Balle: Tabus in der Sprache. 1990.

Band 11 Michael Dunker: Beeinflussung und Steuerung des Lesers in der englischsprachigen Detektiv- und Kriminalliteratur. Eine vergleichende Untersuchung zur Beziehung Autor-Text-Leser in Werken von Doyle, Christie und Highsmith. 1991.

Band 12 Hjördis Jendryschik: Afrikanische Bauformen des Erzählens. Spezifische Eigenarten des frankophonen Romans Schwarzafrikas. 1991.

Band 13 Martin Forstner (Hrsg.): Festgabe für Hans-Rudolf Singer. Zum 65. Geburtstag am 6. April 1990 überreicht von seinen Freunden und Kollegen. 1991.

Band 14 Marcellinus Edorh: Theater in Ghana. Weltsicht, Rituale, Mythen, Tanzdrama, „Social drama", „Ananse sem", „Comic plays" und moderne Dramen. 1991.

Band 15 Martin Forstner / Klaus von Schilling (Hrsg.): Interdisziplinarität. Deutsche Sprache und Literatur im Spannungsfeld der Kulturen. Festschrift für Gerhart Mayer zum 65. Geburtstag. 1991.

Band 16 Anthony Pym: Translation and Text Transfer. An Essay on the Principles of Intercultural Communication. 1992.

Band 17 Harald Nelson: Die Sprache französischer Schüler. Schulspezifische Designate und ihre Bezeichnung. 1994.

Band 18 Karl-Heinz Stoll: Postmoderner Feminismus: Caryl Churchills Dramen. 1995.

Band 19 Nikolai Salnikow (Hrsg.): Sprachtransfer – Kulturtransfer. Text, Kontext und Translation. 1995.

Band 20 Peter P. Konder / Matthias Perl / Klaus Pörtl (Hrsg.): Estudios de literatura y cultura colombianas y de lingüística afro-hispánica. 1995.

Band 21 Heike Jüngst: Frauengestalten und Frauenthemen bei John Arden und Margaretta D'Arcy. Mit Vergleichskapiteln zu Ann Jellicoe, Arnold Wesker, John McGrath und Caryl Churchill. 1996.

Band 22 Andreas F. Kelletat (Hrsg.): Übersetzerische Kompetenz. Beiträge zur universitären Übersetzerausbildung in Deutschland und Skandinavien. 1996.

Band 23 Horst W. Drescher (Hrsg.): Transfer. Übersetzen – Dolmetschen – Interkulturalität. 50 Jahre Fachbereich Angewandte Sprach- und Kulturwissenschaft der Johannes Gutenberg-Universität Mainz in Germersheim. 1997.

Band 24 Dieter Huber / Erika Worbs (Hrsg.): Ars transferendi – Sprache, Übersetzung, Interkulturalität. Festschrift für Nikolai Salnikow zum 65. Geburtstag. 1998.

Band 25 Cornelia Weege: Bild und Rolle der Frau im dramatischen Werk von José Martín Recuerda. 1999.

Band 26 Eva Katrin Müller: Sprachwahl im spanisch-deutschen Sprachkontakt in Südchile. Ergebnisse einer sprachsoziologischen Untersuchung unter Nachfahren deutscher Einwanderer. 2000.

Band 27 Sabine Rommer: L'Inde perdue. Französische Kolonialromane des 19. und 20. Jahrhunderts über Indien. 2001.

Band 28 Stefan Barme: Der Subjektausdruck beim Verb in phonisch-nähesprachlichen Varietäten des europäischen Portugiesisch und Brasilianischen. 2001.

Band 29 Holger Siever: Kommunikation und Verstehen. Der Fall Jenninger als Beispiel einer semiotischen Kommunikationsanalyse. 2001.

Band 30 Andreas F. Kelletat (Hrsg.): Dolmetschen. Beiträge aus Forschung, Lehre und Praxis. 2001.

Band 31 Iris Plack: Die deutschsprachige Rezeption von Luigi Pirandellos Bühnenwerk. 2002.

Band 32 Britta Nord: Hilfsmittel beim Übersetzen. Eine empirische Studie zum Rechercheverhalten professioneller Übersetzer. 2002.

Band 33 Christian Todenhagen / Wolfgang Thiele (eds.): Investigations into Narrative Structures. 2002.

Band 34 Dörte Andres: Konsekutivdolmetschen und Notation. 2002.

Band 35 Matthias Perl / Klaus Pörtl (eds.): Estudios de lingüística hispanoamericana, brasileña y criolla. 2002.

Band 36 „Die ganze Welt ist Bühne" / „Todo el mundo es un escenario". Festschrift für Klaus Pörtl zum 65. Geburtstag / Homenaje a Klaus Pörtl en ocasión de su 65 aniversario. Herausgegeben von / Editado por Matthias Perl und / y Wolfgang Pöckl. 2003.

Band 37 Ângela Maria Pereira Nunes: Vergangenheitsbewältigung im interkulturellen Transfer. Zur Aufarbeitung europäischer Geschichte in José Saramagos O Ano da Morte de Ricardo Reis. 2003.

Band 38 Rainer Kohlmayer / Wolfgang Pöckl (Hrsg.): Literarisches und mediales Übersetzen. Aufsätze zu Theorie und Praxis einer gelehrten Kunst. 2004.

Band 39 Matthias Vollet / Felipe Castañeda (Hrsg.): Mission und Sprache. Interdisziplinäre Erkundungen zum Orden Colonial in Iberoamerika. 2004.

Band 40 Vito Lo Scrudato: L'ultimo brigante. Nel latifondo siciliano tra '800 e '900. 2004.

Band 41 Barbara Ahrens: Prosodie beim Simultandolmetschen. 2004.

Band 42 Klaus Pörtl: Panorámica del teatro español y latinoamericano del siglo XX. 2004.

Band 43 Araceli Marín Presno: Zur Rezeption der Novelle *Rinconete y Cortadillo* von Miguel de Cervantes im deutschsprachigen Raum. 2005.

Band 44 Rebekka Bratschi: Xenismen in der Werbung. Die Instrumentalisierung des Fremden. 2005.

Band 45 Katrin Buchta / Andreas Guder (Hrsg.): China.Literatur.Übersetzen. Beiträge eines Symposiums zu Ehren von Ulrich Kautz. 2006.

Band 46 Wolfgang Pöckl / Michael Schreiber (Hrsg.): Geschichte und Gegenwart der Übersetzung im französischen Sprachraum. 2008.

Band 47 Peter Kupfer (ed.): Youtai – Presence and Perception of Jews and Judaism in China. 2008.

Band 48 Athanasios Anastasiadis: Der Norden im Süden. Kostantinos Chatzopoulos (1868-1920) als Übersetzer deutscher Literatur. 2008.

Band 49 Michael Poerner: Business-Knigge China. Die Darstellung Chinas in interkultureller Ratgeberliteratur. 2009.

Band 50 Barbara Ahrens / Lothar Černý / Monika Krein-Kühle / Michael Schreiber (Hrsg.): Translationswissenschaftliches Kolloquium I. Beiträge zur Übersetzungs- und Dolmetschwissenschaft (Köln/Germersheim). 2009.

Band 51 Konstantina Glykioti / Doris Kinne (Hrsg.): Griechisch – Ελληνικά – Grekiska: Festschrift für Hans Ruge. 2009.

Band 52 Judith Schreier: Der Piropo als Instrument verbaler Interaktion. Eine soziopragmatische Untersuchung am Beispiel Venezuelas. 2009.

Band 53 Aiga Dukāte: Translation, Manipulation and Interpreting. 2009.

Band 54 Erika Worbs (Hrsg.): Neue Zeiten – neue Wörter – neue Wörterbücher. Beiträge zur Neologismenlexikografie und -lexikologie. 2009.

Band 55 Stefan Feihl: Resultativkonstruktionen mit Prädikatsadjektiv und ihre Übersetzung aus dem Deutschen ins Französische, Italienische, Spanische und Portugiesische. 2009.

Band 56 Владислава В. Жданова/Vladislava Ždanova: „Нашим оружием было слово...". Переводчики на войне. „Unsere Waffe war das Wort...". Translation in Kriegszeiten. 2009.

Band 57 Dennis Scheller-Boltz: Präponeme und Präponemkonstrukte im Russischen, Polnischen und Deutschen. Zur Terminologie, Morphologie und Semantik einer Wortbildungseinheit und eines produktiven Kompositionstypus. 2010.

Band 58 Doris Kinne: Untersuchungen zur Morphologie des Verbs in griechischen Pressetexten unter dem Aspekt der Bistrukturalität. 2011.

Band 59 Cornelia Schindelin / Michael Poerner (Hrsg.): Sprache und Genuss. Beiträge des Symposiums zu Ehren von Peter Kupfer. 2012.

Band 60 Barbara Ahrens / Silvia Hansen-Schirra / Monika Krein-Kühle / Michael Schreiber / Ursula Wienen (Hrsg.): Translationswissenschaftliches Kolloquium II. Beiträge zur Übersetzungs- und Dolmetschwissenschaft (Köln/Germersheim). 2012.

Band 61 Silvia Hansen-Schirra / Don Kiraly (Hrsg.): Projekte und Projektionen in der translatorischen Kompetenzentwicklung. 2013.

Band 62 Silvia Hansen-Schirra / Karin Maksymski (eds.): Aviation Communications. Between Theory and Practice. 2013.

REIHE B - Studientexte

Band 1 Ph. Woolley: The Queen's English. Exercises in the Pronounciation of English. 1974. 2. Auflage. 1976. 3. überarbeitete Auflage. 1982.

Band 2 K.-P. Lange: Kurzgefaßte Einführung in die Generative Syntax. 1975.

Band 4 Michalis Kanavakis: Griechisch für Deutsche. Teil 1. 1986. 2. unveränderte Auflage. 1987.

www.peterlang.de

www.ingramcontent.com/pod-product-compliance
Ingram Content Group UK Ltd.
Pitfield, Milton Keynes, MK11 3LW, UK
UKHW022154230426
12049UKWH00004BA/88